Cambridge Elements

Elements in International Law and Society
edited by
Richard Clements
Tilburg University
Luis Eslava
La Trobe University
Markus Gunneflo
Lund University
Nadia Lambek
Western University

TOWARD AN ABOLITIONIST HUMAN RIGHTS COURT

Rethinking Responses to Gendered and Racialized Violence

Karen Engle
University of Texas School of Law

CAMBRIDGE
UNIVERSITY PRESS

Shaftesbury Road, Cambridge CB2 8EA, United Kingdom

One Liberty Plaza, 20th Floor, New York, NY 10006, USA

477 Williamstown Road, Port Melbourne, VIC 3207, Australia

314–321, 3rd Floor, Plot 3, Splendor Forum, Jasola District Centre, New Delhi – 110025, India

103 Penang Road, #05–06/07, Visioncrest Commercial, Singapore 238467

Cambridge University Press is part of Cambridge University Press & Assessment, a department of the University of Cambridge.

We share the University's mission to contribute to society through the pursuit of education, learning and research at the highest international levels of excellence.

www.cambridge.org
Information on this title: www.cambridge.org/9781009690133

DOI: 10.1017/9781009690157

© Karen Engle 2025

This publication is in copyright. Subject to statutory exception and to the provisions of relevant collective licensing agreements, no reproduction of any part may take place without the written permission of Cambridge University Press & Assessment.

When citing this work, please include a reference to the DOI 10.1017/9781009690157

First published 2025

A catalogue record for this publication is available from the British Library

ISBN 978-1-009-69013-3 Hardback
ISBN 978-1-009-69012-6 Paperback
ISSN 3050-2896 (online)
ISSN 3050-2888 (print)

Cambridge University Press & Assessment has no responsibility for the persistence or accuracy of URLs for external or third-party internet websites referred to in this publication and does not guarantee that any content on such websites is, or will remain, accurate or appropriate.

For EU product safety concerns, contact us at Calle de José Abascal, 56, 1°, 28003 Madrid, Spain, or email eugpsr@cambridge.org

Toward an Abolitionist Human Rights Court

Rethinking Responses to Gendered and Racialized Violence

Elements in International Law and Society

DOI: 10.1017/9781009690157
First published online: May 2025

Karen Engle
University of Texas School of Law
Author for correspondence: Karen Engle, kengle@law.utexas.edu

> **Abstract:** Contemporary international human rights law increasingly obligates states to heighten their criminalization of certain human rights violations, including gendered, racialized, and homophobic violence. This Element uses prison and police abolitionist thought to challenge this trend. It focuses on the European Court of Human Rights (ECtHR), arguing that the Court's reliance on punishment and policing threatens to undo earlier European approaches to criminal law and human rights that resonate with abolitionist thought. It also contends that the criminalization approach provides the Court with an alibi for not recognizing or attending to the deeply structural racialized, colonial, sexual, gendered, and homophobic violence in Europe, particularly but not only against Roma communities and Black and Muslim migrants. Encouraging human rights advocates and judges to take seriously prison and police abolition in Europe and elsewhere, the Element calls for the ECtHR to pave the way for an abolitionist-oriented turn among human rights courts.

Keywords: racial justice, gender justice, human rights, hate crimes, European Court of Human Rights

© Karen Engle 2025

ISBNs: 9781009690133 (HB), 9781009690126 (PB), 9781009690157 (OC)
ISSNs: 3050-2896 (online), 3050-2888 (print)

Contents

1 Introduction   1

2 Human Rights and Abolitionist Movements: Resonances and Dissonances   4

3 Jurisprudence on Gendered and Racialized Violence   20

4 Sketching the Contours of an Abolitionist Human Rights Court   48

5 Conclusion   58

References   60

1 Introduction

This Element considers the (in)compatibility of movements for prison and police abolition with human rights law, movements, and discourse. It is centered on a largely unstated and even unrecognized tension: While some of the most vocal abolitionists have long considered human rights to be central to their aims, most human rights advocates have not prioritized or even supported prison or police abolition. The two groups, of course, agree on many matters and often see each other as allies. For instance, both oppose police abuse, the death penalty, and mass incarceration. Yet they view the causes of and responses to these issues quite differently. While abolitionists refuse the ideologies and practices of the carceral state, human rights advocates – particularly over the past two decades – have come to depend upon them to back up their anti-impunity rallying cry. Indeed, human rights advocates have had tremendous success in defining anti-impunity in criminal punishment terms – not only by helping to establish new international criminal institutions but by embedding a penal response to human rights violations in human rights institutions, international and regional (Cavallaro and O'Connell 2020; Engle 2015; Engle, Miller, and Davis 2016; Huneeus 2013; Lavrysen and Mavronicola 2020; Mégret and Calderón 2015; Seibert-Fohr 2009).

As part of a larger project considering the resonances and dissonances between abolition, on one hand, and human rights law and practice, on the other, this Element uses penal abolitionist thought to critique the jurisprudence of the European Court of Human Rights (ECtHR). Established in the 1950s by the European Convention on Human Rights (ECHR), the Court today adjudicates claims of violations of the Convention, primarily brought by individuals, against Council of Europe member states, which are all parties to the Convention.[1] Through an abolitionist lens, I encourage the Court and advocates bringing or supporting claims before the Court to break away from the dominant carceral trend in human rights law and advocacy, largely by expanding their remedial imagination. To make my argument, I focus on two areas where the Court has been the most anti-abolitionist and yet the least critiqued: cases involving gender-based (including sexual) violence and those regarding racist, homophobic, and transphobic hate crimes. I refer to these forms of violence collectively as gendered and racialized violence.

I concentrate on Europe and the ECtHR for several reasons that I elaborate throughout the Element. To begin, Europe is far from immune to racialized

---

[1] Only since 1998, with Protocol No. 11, has the European Convention required all member states to be subject to individual complaints before the ECtHR. Previously, states were subject to interstate complaints but could choose whether to consent both to individual petitions and the jurisdiction of the Court (as opposed to the now-defunct European Commission of Human Rights).

violence, including as it intersects with gendered and homophobic violence. As cases before the Court demonstrate, Roma communities and racialized migrants often bear the brunt of that violence, including by state actors. Further, early theories of and movements toward penal abolition in the 1970s mostly emerged from Europe, largely in the context of prisoners' rights. Many of those theories have informed contemporary abolitionist thought and movements not only in Europe but in other parts of the world, principally the United States. At the same time, US abolitionist literature and movements have taken the lead in theorizing the ongoing racialized and gendered effects of relying upon policing and prisons, making their critiques particularly relevant to the ECtHR case law I consider.

In addition, and perhaps related to the history of abolitionist thought in Europe, many countries in Europe, as well as the Council of Europe as a whole, have achieved significant penal reforms. While some have their roots in penal minimalism,[2] in which criminal law is seen as the *ultima ratio*, or last resort, many are or have the potential to be what abolitionists consider "non-reformist" reforms, or those reforms that go "beyond the facilities and presuppositions" of the prevailing penal system (Mathiesen [1974] 2015: 231). Over the years, the ECtHR has played a role in, even instigated, some of those changes.

Notwithstanding this history, the ECtHR has been swept up in the broader global wave of human rights law and activism that demands criminal punishment for "serious human rights violations."[3] Even while insisting both that it has a limited mandate and that it is not a criminal court, the ECtHR often finds that states have positive obligations to respond criminally, sometimes with enhanced penalties, to a range of human rights violations.

These judgments – some of which former ECtHR judge Françoise Tulkens (2011) has identified as the Court's deployment of the sword function of criminal law in human rights, as opposed to its shield function – have increased

---

[2] For discussion of the history of penal minimalism, traced to Italian philosopher Luigi Ferrajoli in the 1970s, as well as some of the agreements, historical and contemporary, between penal abolitionists and penal minimalists, see Langer 2020: 54–56. For discussion of the Continental, principally German, application of *ultima ratio*, or last resort, to criminal law, see Peršak 2020: 143–147.

[3] The term "serious human rights violations" is often used but rarely defined or is defined in a circular manner to mean human rights violations that require a criminal law response. As Rachel Lopez (2020: 569) puts it, speaking of the interchangeability and lack of definition of the terms "serious," "grave," and "gross" to modify human rights: "To a large extent, gravity has become the 'I know it when I see it' of international law." The Council of Europe has proffered a definition of serious human rights violations in its Guidelines on Eradicating Impunity for Serious Human Rights Violations, which centers on violations of Articles 2, 3, 4, 5(1), and 5, while noting that "not all violations of these articles will necessarily reach this threshold" (Directorate General of Human Rights & Rule of Law 2011: 7).

over time and threaten to undo some of the Court's own achievements regarding penal reform. Invoking penal minimalism, she explained in 2011 that "it appears that the reserved and essentially negative obligation to use the criminal law only as a last resort is being replaced, at least in part, by a positive obligation to favour it and to implement it in practical terms" (594). As she put it more recently (Tulkens 2020: vi–vii), "the state is now accountable *not for having used* criminal law, but for *not having used it* or having used it with too much leniency."

At the same time, the case law facilitates the Court's *claims* to take seriously certain human rights violations. Especially alongside often rhetorical assertions of deterrence, the imposition of positive obligations on states to police and punish provides the Court with an alibi for not calling for the type of meaningful structural redress that abolitionists insist on.

While a number of scholars have usefully mapped the application of these obligations, which Laurens Lavrysen and Natasa Mavronicola (2020) refer to as "coercive human rights," they have not brought an abolitionist lens to their work to propose alternative, non-penal approaches that the Court might take. They also have not recognized the extent to which the Court has placed positive obligations on states to increase or better equip their police force.

This Element aims to fill these lacunae. Specifically, it challenges human rights law and advocacy that claim to be grounded in gender and racial justice to take seriously the racialized and gendered inequities that (over)criminalization and (over)policing produce and reproduce. Beyond fortifying the traditional shield of human rights, I argue, judges and advocates should channel both their condemnation of particular forms of violence and their commitment to hold states accountable for that violence in ways that facilitate the pursuit of alternative, non-penal approaches to the adjudication of serious human rights violations. Specifically, the ECtHR should replace its imposition of positive obligations on states to police and punish with non-penal reparative remedies, including positive obligations to achieve structural change. Encouraging states to seek non-penal responses to human rights violations would, at a minimum, bring the Court into alignment with its jurisprudence that makes criminal punishment a last resort.

In what follows, Section 2 identifies historical and contemporary resonances and dissonances between the movements for human rights and abolition, particularly but not only in the context of Europe. Section 3 sets forth and brings prison and police abolitionist lenses to the ECtHR case law that imposes positive obligations on states to use criminal law to punish, often with heightened sanctions and increased policing, gender-based violence as well as hate crimes motivated by racism, homophobia, and transphobia. In Section 4, I urge the ECtHR to lead the way for an abolitionist turn by human rights institutions and advocacy, in part by returning to its roots as a human rights (not criminal) court. I propose a variety of non-penal positive obligations that the Court could impose on states that would cement its commitment to address the structural causes and harms of gendered and racialized violence committed by both state and non-state actors. I also propose ways that the Court can ensure redress and other support for victims of that violence as well as spur non-reformist penal reforms more generally.

2 Human Rights and Abolitionist Movements: Resonances and Dissonances

2.1 Abolition, Reform, and Human Rights

The penal abolition movement emerged, mostly in Europe, around the same time as the contemporary human rights movement. The two movements shared a number of concerns from near the beginning, particularly with regard to the uses of incarceration and the treatment of prisoners.

In the 1960s and 1970s, long before they turned to criminal law as their principal enforcement mechanism, human rights law and movements were largely in line with what David Garland (2001) identifies as the penal welfarism that was dominant at the time. That is, they focused largely on due process rights for the accused, prison conditions, and even on getting people out of prison. Due process and the prohibition on torture and inhuman or degrading treatment and punishment were enshrined in all major human rights legal instruments from the beginning. The International Covenant on Civil and Political Rights even circumscribed the use of prisons to the purposes of "reformation and social rehabilitation,"[4] precluding the justifications of deterrence and retribution that, as I discuss in Section 4.2, are the two rationales most commonly stated or presumed by human rights advocates today.

When Amnesty International (AI) began its work in 1961 with letter-writing campaigns calling for the release of prisoners, it distinguished between political and other prisoners, advocating only on behalf of those it deemed "prisoners of conscience," meaning those who had not advocated or condoned violence (Benenson 1961). As early as 1964, however, it began scrutinizing the criminal justice system's treatment of all political prisoners, even if it chose not to work

---

[4] International Covenant on Civil and Political Rights (ICCPR) Art. 10(3), Dec. 16, 1966, 999 UNTS 171. The ICCPR General Comment No. 21 in 1992 interpreted the ICCPR as prohibiting a penitentiary system that was "only retributory," requiring that "it should essentially seek the reformation and social rehabilitation of the prisoner." United Nations Human Rights Committee, General Comment No. 21: Article 10 (Humane treatment of persons deprived of their liberty), para. 10 (Apr. 10, 1992), available from: https://perma.cc/7M8X-3WBU.

for the release of those who advocated force, including Nelson Mandela (Amnesty International 1965: 7; Mandela 1995: 612). In 1968, while maintaining its stance on calling only for the release of prisoners of conscience, AI officially expanded its mandate to consider the treatment of all prisoners, political and otherwise. In doing so it relied on the Universal Declaration of Human Rights, in particular Article 5 prohibiting torture and cruel and inhumane punishment and Article 9 prohibiting arbitrary arrest and detention (Amnesty International 1970: 1; Wong 2012: 208). Opposition to the death penalty became part of AI's mandate in the early 1970s. Thus, while the organization might have found the criminal punishment systems of some states more suspect than others, it saw all countries as capable of abusing their penal power.

Although penal abolitionists during the same period explicitly called for an end to the prison system in a way that the human rights movement did not, they relied on similar evidence and analysis about the cruel and degrading nature of incarceration. Many abolitionists were closely connected to and often directly involved with prisoners' movements that focused on improving the conditions of imprisonment because, as the early and influential Norwegian penal abolitionist Thomas Mathiesen (2015: xv) put it, "even criminals had to have decent lives and human rights." Mathiesen attributed the creation of grassroots prisoner organizations across Western Europe, including KROM in Norway with which he worked closely, to 1968 radicalism (Mathiesen 2015: 9). Many of those organizations, including KROM, would soon call for prison abolition.

Questions of human rights were therefore at the heart of a debate among abolitionists that remains today: Should those who argue for abolition in the long term support or even promote, in the short term, the more humane treatment of prisoners? Perhaps because of his work with KROM, Mathiesen was preoccupied with this issue. In the 1970s (Mathiesen [1974] 2015), he began distinguishing between those reforms that he considered "negative," or abolitionist, and those that he considered "positive" (223). The latter, which he opposed, are "changes which improve or 'build up' the system so that it functions more effectively – whereby the system is strengthened and its abolition made more difficult," partly due to "the renewed legitimacy which an improvement bestows on the system" (emphasis omitted). In contrast, "negative" reforms, which Mathiesen supported, "are changes which abolish or remove greater or smaller parts on which the system in general is more or less dependent" (223, emphasis omitted).

Two examples of proposed reforms that Mathiesen discussed to work through his analysis are increasing the number of treatment staff in prisons and building new prisons that, through architectural changes, allow for more freedom of movement. He insisted that both are positive reforms, the former because the "treatment orientation" both "confers legitimacy on the prison as a solution to crime as an inter-human problem" and produces reforms that "are absorbed by the prison system in such a way that the prisoner benefits little or nothing from them" (224). The latter is also a positive reform because the new prisons come with new technologies of surveillance that neutralize any negative effect that might have been achieved (226). Mathiesen acknowledged that even "[a] negative reform may soften public criticism, and thereby in a way improve the system's basis of legitimacy .... But the negative, abolishing reform does not provide the system with a new, positive addition of legitimacy" (223).

Mathiesen connected his contrast between positive and negative/abolitionist reforms with the work of sociologist André Gorz, who wrote of "reformist" versus "non-reformist" reforms in the labor context. For Gorz, Mathiesen explained, "'[r]eformist' reforms have goals which are subordinated to the facilities and the presuppositions of a system and a policy presented by the adversary." A non-reformist reform, in contrast, "is not geared to whatever is possible within the framework of a given system, but to that which 'should be realizable' in view of human demands and needs" (231, citing Gorz 1964). Although Mathiesen considered many of Gorz's non-reformist reforms in fact to be positive (or reformist) reforms, he adopted the language: "Another way of stating this is to say that in order to be what Gorz calls 'non-reformist' – in order to break with the presuppositions of the main system – a reform must be of the abolishing kind" (Mathiesen [1974] 2015: 232, emphasis omitted).

Mathiesen and KROM were not alone in experiencing the potential incompatibility of advocating for prisoners' rights and calling for penal abolition. A similar tension emerged in the UK in the early 1970s, with the abolitionist group Radical Alternatives to Prison (RAP) sharply distinguishing itself from Preservation of the Rights of Prisoners (PROP), a prisoners' union that formed around the same time. Distancing itself from what it labeled PROP's "short-term reformist goals," RAP criticized members of PROP for their seeming belief "that prisons are an inevitable part of the social system" (Ryan and Ward 2014: 109, quoting RAP statement from Ryan 1978: 113). In contrast, RAP proposed alternatives to incarceration that "would be based on much greater community participation and would also encompass radical changes in ... society" (Ryan and Ward 2014: 109). Importantly, RAP did engage in some arguably non-reformist reforms, such as opposing the employment of more prison psychiatrists and campaigning for an end to prison censorship. At the same time, internal debates ensued within RAP as to whether some of its own community-based alternatives to imprisonment also depended upon coercion (Ryan and Ward, 2014: 109–111).

I have discussed at some length this distinction between reformist and non-reformist reforms because it guides much of my analysis of the ECtHR case law throughout this Element. The distinction has had incredible staying power for police and prison abolitionists, who see abolition not as a utopian ideal but as a process or, as Mathiesen ([1974] 2015: 47–62) put it, perpetually "unfinished." Leading US abolitionist thinkers Ruth Wilson Gilmore and Craig Gilmore (2008: 145), for instance, cite Gorz and Mathiesen in their consideration of whether particular reforms support the carceral state (and are thus reformist reforms) or instead entail "systemic changes that do not extend the life or breadth of deadly forces such as prisons." For Angela Davis, Gina Dent, Erica Meiners, and Beth Richie (2022: 36), who also cite both Mathiesen and Gorz, non-reformist reforms are those "that make sustainable and material differences in the lives of people under the control of oppressive systems."

Even though the distinction is commonly used today by prison and police abolitionists (for example, Critical Resistance 2020a; Kaba 2014) and it was first articulated in response to a perceived tension between abolition and prisoners' human rights, it has received little attention among human rights advocates. And while human rights law and advocacy have become more reliant on criminal law for its enforcement over time, abolitionists today engage in less hand-wringing than their predecessors over whether supporting human rights work is reformist, generally accepting human rights advocacy as important to their abolitionist struggles.

The Routledge International Handbook of Penal Abolition (Coyle and Scott 2021) demonstrates some of this contemporary approach to human rights by abolitionists. The volume contains chapters written by abolitionist academics and advocates from around the world, some of whom are described in their short biographies in the book as working in human rights. Several chapters situate abolitionist movements that the authors consider to be within the human rights movement. Tellingly, the index states, at the end of nearly an entire column of entries on abolitionism, "see also human rights" (459).

The chapter by Debbie Kilroy and Suzi Quixley (2021) on Sisters Inside in Australia, which Kilroy founded in 1992, provides an example. It begins with a history of the organization, which the authors describe as "an independent community organization in Queensland, Australia, that advocates for the collective human rights of criminalized women and girls and provides services to meet their own and their children's needs" (23). Kilroy and Quixley describe the organization's "transformation from a reformist to an abolitionist organization" (22) in a way that demonstrates that human rights have been central to both sides of that transformation. Much of the group's work has involved bringing complaints about conditions in women's prisons to national and international human rights institutions and calling for national human rights legislation in Australia (26–28). When Sisters Inside first articulated its abolitionist position in 2007, it did so in a guide that "provided practical steps to implement a human rights-based approach to organizational and service development" (27).

Another chapter in the collection discusses a feminist group in Asturias, Spain (Coleutivu Milenta Muyeres, or Milenta Group), whose work also includes advocating for the conditions of women in prison. According to the chapter's authors, the organization considers itself to be abolitionist and "pronounces that prisons go against all basic human rights and are a place of suffering and deterioration" (Francés Lecumberri and Restrepo Rodríguez 2021: 155).

Ironically, even in the United States, where human rights carry relatively little legal weight, abolitionists often deploy human rights. Angela Y. Davis, for instance, has long framed abolition as a human rights issue, including by relying in her 2003 book *Are Prisons Obsolete?* on Human Rights Watch reports from the 1990s on prison conditions in the United States (Davis 2003: 49–50, 77, 101–102). The more recent Movement for Black Lives has not only deployed the language of human rights but brought human rights complaints to the United Nations about racist police violence as one means of supporting its calls for police abolition (Achiume 2020).

Some of the reliance on human rights among abolitionists in the United States can be traced to African American activism that has long turned to human rights, even or especially over civil rights, to bring the world's attention to the deep structural legacies of slavery. As Carol Anderson (2003) details, in the mid 1940s, the National Negro Congress and later the National Association for the Advancement of Colored People (NAACP), with the help of W. E. B. Du Bois, unsuccessfully petitioned the newly formed United Nations to respond to the economic and political plight of Black Americans. After both the passage of the Genocide Convention and the adoption of the Universal Declaration of Human Rights in 1948, the Civil Rights Congress (1951) attempted to petition the United Nations with a widely distributed document entitled "We Charge Genocide." In 1964, Malcolm X invoked human rights over civil rights, urging Black Americans to take the United States to the "world court" (X 1965: 35). Although abolition was not necessarily a part of that history, Benjamin Weber (2021: 706) has drawn from what he calls the "anticarceral internationalism" of the "imprisoned Black radical tradition" to ground an appeal for a human rights paradigm that would support prison abolition.

Other contemporary abolitionists believe the movement should rely on even more traditional human rights approaches, each for slightly different reasons. For Jonathan Simon (2019: 350) in the United States, abolition will be more likely to succeed if grounded in human dignity than if based in arguments for economic efficiency. For David Scott (2016: 58) in the United Kingdom, abolitionists should "promote human rights as part of their counter-hegemonic strategy."

The human rights that abolitionists deploy or reference often fall into the relatively narrow category of the civil and political rights of prisoners or, in the context of police abolition, suspects and profiled individuals. Abolitionists, though not as explicitly as in the 1970s, treat these rights as necessary in the short term while they work toward the long-term goal of seeing not only the end of the penal system but the end of the *need* for it, in part through the dismantling of racialized and gendered structures that help fuel the prison industrial complex.

Seeing human rights as principally about prisoners' rights, however, misses both a constraining and a potentially liberating strand of human rights activism. As I have already mentioned, abolitionists generally fail to see the reliance of much of contemporary human rights advocacy on criminal law. But they also miss, ironically perhaps, that many in the human rights movement claim a broader commitment – to economic and social rights and, relatedly, to the dismantling of racialized and gendered structural oppression. In other words, were abolitionists to broaden their human rights lens, appealing to the long-term goals that they share with at least some human rights advocates, they could play an important role in disputing human rights' reliance on criminal punishment as a short-term strategy.

This Element aims to facilitate that possibility by highlighting some of the potential impasses and opportunities between abolitionist and human rights aims, including as they sometimes play out *within* human rights. As to the latter, European human rights scholars have identified a tension between the shield and sword functions of criminal law in relation to the ECtHR's jurisprudence. Were they to approach the tension through an abolitionist lens, they would acknowledge that the two functions cannot simply live alongside each other. To return to Mathiesen ([1974] 2015: 231):

> [T]he short-term reforms which you work for – have to work for – as a road to the long-term goal of abolition must be of a very specific type: they must also consistently be of an abolishing kind. Only then – by a stubborn insistence on abolition also in what is close at hand – do you have a chance to solve the conflict between short-term and long-term objectives.

To move in an abolitionist direction, the ECtHR should therefore, in the short term, reject the Court's use of criminal law as a sword and bolster the human rights shield to promote non-reformist penal reforms. In the long term, it should work toward the elimination of the need for the shield altogether, in part by addressing the structural roots of those very harms that it currently claims to address with the sword.

Before delving into some of the ECtHR jurisprudence that demonstrates the Court's reliance on the sword function in responding to racialized and gendered violence, I turn to some resonances and dissonances between human rights and prison and police abolition that can be found within the Council of Europe, including in much of the ECtHR's jurisprudence. I will draw further on and expand upon some of the resonances in Section 4.2.

2.2 Prison Abolition and the Council of Europe

Prison abolitionists in Council of Europe member states might see human rights law as aligned with their aims for some of the same reasons I already outlined. Specific to the Council of Europe, the ECHR, which is the oldest regional human rights treaty, enshrines the rights of the accused, particularly those found in Article 2 (right to life), Article 3 (prohibition of torture and inhuman or degrading treatment), Article 5 (right to liberty and security), Article 6 (right to a fair trial), Article 7 (no punishment without law), Article 8 (right to privacy), Article 10 (free expression), and Article 14 (prohibition of discrimination).

With regard to prisoners' rights, the ECtHR has ruled against states for the physical assault and mistreatment of prisoners (including lack of attention to medical needs). It has also found incarcerated individuals entitled to a broad range of civil and political rights, including freedom of thought, conscience, and religion; freedom of expression; the right to vote; and the prohibition of discrimination, including the requirement of accommodations for people with disabilities. Further, it has found states in violation of the Convention for failing to provide individuals who are incarcerated with family and personal visits, treatment for substance use disorder, proper renumeration for work, and, most recently, gender-affirming care.[5]

The Council of Europe and the ECtHR have also used the Convention to engage in or precipitate significant penal reforms, some arguably non-reformist. Scholars have pointed to specific articles of the Convention, along with some of the ECtHR's jurisprudence interpreting them, as evidence of the shield function of human rights law (for example, Dumortier et al. 2011; Tulkens 2011). I outline in this section some of the approaches of and actions by the Council of Europe and the ECtHR that resonate with prison abolitionist aims. Most involve interpretation of Articles 2, 3, and 8.

Although penal abolitionists might applaud some of these resonances, it would be a mistake to assume that the reforms are all non-reformist. Though,

---

[5] For a discussion of some of the relevant case law and rights, see European Court of Human Rights 2024b; Wallace 2020; and Wild 2016.

as we have already seen, abolitionists at times disagree on what does and does not fit into the non-reformist category, their insistence on the distinction between the two types provides a useful lens for analyzing the effects of the reforms, in some instances with the advantage of hindsight. Following each potential resonance, I therefore point to some dissonances.

2.2.1 Decriminalization

Decriminalization is an obvious focus of prison abolition and was seriously engaged with by the Council of Europe in the 1970s and 1980s. As Mattia Pinto (2023) recounts, the Council published a *Report on Decriminalisation* in 1980, which was drafted by the Select Committee of Experts on Decriminalisation, chaired by prominent Dutch penal abolitionist Louk Hulsman (European Committee on Crime Problems 1980). According to Pinto (2023), Hulsman's "belief that crimes have no ontological reality but differ from non-criminalised social problems only due to their labelling as such, underpins the whole Report" (1119). In general, "[t]he Report analysed the costs of criminal justice; placed the decriminalization of certain offences within a broader penal abolitionist perspective; and made suggestions on how to overcome the possible dysfunctions that would arise from abolishing or curtailing criminal regulation" (1111). The report was also part of a larger effort to harmonize criminal law and procedure among the member states of the Council of Europe (1110).

Consistent with the decriminalization report, the ECtHR led the way on decriminalization in at least one area. In 1981, in *Dudgeon v. The United Kingdom*, the Court found that the criminalization of sodomy violated Article 8 of the ECHR.[6] The decision is widely seen as pathbreaking, marking the first decision of a human rights body to require the decriminalization of same-sex sexual conduct. In subsequent cases brought against Ireland and Cyprus, the Court made clear that simply not enforcing a law that remains on the books is insufficient; the existence of a statute that criminalizes same-sex sexual conduct violates the Convention.[7]

Unfortunately from an abolitionist perspective, sodomy has turned out to be one of the few instances in which the ECtHR has required decriminalization and, as Pinto (2023: 1118) points out, the 1980 report "was soon all but forgotten." Contrary to the harmonizing approach of the report, the Court has largely invoked its margin of appreciation doctrine – granting states a wide degree of latitude in their interpretation of the Convention – to justify its lack of

---

[6] *Dudgeon v. The United Kingdom*, App. No. 7525/76 (Eur. Ct. H. R. Oct. 22, 1981).
[7] *Norris v. Ireland*, App. No. 10581/83 (Eur. Ct. H. R. Oct. 26, 1988); *Modinos v. Cyprus*, App. No. 15070/89 (Eur. Ct. H. R. Apr. 22, 1993).

intervention, even in the context of other sexual conduct, both personal and commercial.

On several ocassions, the Court has allowed states to criminalize conduct that they see as harmful, even sometimes against the stated desires of those considered to be victims. In a series of cases since 1997 against the UK and Belgium, the Court has rejected challenges to the criminalization of group sex and sadomasochism (Gilleri 2023: 56–80). More recently, the Court ruled unanimously against sex workers in France who complained that the state's criminalization of the purchase of sex violated the ECHR. Granting France a broad margin of appreciation, the Court insisted that, particularly given the lack of consensus among member states and the "delicate" moral questions involved, the French state is "better placed than the international judge to pronounce not only on the 'precise content of the demands of morality' but also on the need for a restriction intended to address it."[8] At the same time, the Court noted that all parties to the litigation were in support of France's 2015 abolition of the criminalization of the *provision* of sex work. While a favorable reference to the decriminalization of solicitation might sound as though it resonates with abolitionist approaches, the Court used it as a means of deferring to France's presumption that sex workers will be more likely to report to police if their own acts of solicitation are not criminalized. Indeed, encouraging them to report would be useful for the challenged legislation, which also increases criminal sanctions for violence against sex workers, whom the Court names as vulnerable victims.[9]

Pointing to the Court's 1976 decision in *Engel and Others* v. *Netherlands*, which read the Convention as leaving "States free to designate as a criminal offence any act or omission not constituting the normal exercise of one of the rights it protects," Pinto (2023: 1111–1113) observes that the ECtHR situates itself in a way that limits its ability to respond to overcriminalization.[10] He identifies defamation (on which he focuses) and abortion as two areas in which the Court has refused to find that human rights require decriminalization, even though some UN treaty bodies have reached contrary decisions (1116). He also notes that some UN treaty bodies have been critical of the criminalization of a range of conduct that has not been taken up by the ECtHR, including adultery, drug possession, apostacy, vagrancy, and land occupation (1116).

---

[8] *M. A. and Others* v. *France*, App. No. 63664/19 (Eur. Ct. H.R. Jul. 25, 2024), para. 147 (translation; original: "les autorités de l'État se trouvent en principe mieux placées que le juge international pour se prononcer non seulement sur le 'contenu précis des exigences de la morale' mais aussi sur la nécessité d'une restriction destinée à y répondre").

[9] *M. A. and Others* v. *France*, para. 161.

[10] Quoting *Engel and Others* v. *Netherlands*, App. Nos. 5100/71, 5101/71, 5102/71, 5354/72, and 5370/72, para. 81 (Eur. Ct. H.R. Jun. 8, 1976).

Of course, the ECtHR's failure to require the decriminalization of abortion, defamation, or the purchase of sex is tied up with its refusal to recognize the conduct as protected by ECHR rights. At the same time, the Court's approach prevents it from evaluating the question whether criminalization is an appropriate response not only in these areas but, as Steven Malby (2019: 169–170) has pointed out, in more "trivial" areas as well.

2.2.2 The Death Penalty and Life Without Parole (Irreducible Life Sentences)

Abolitionists have pointed to ending the death penalty as an abolitionist "turning point" (Mathiesen 2015: 34–35). And human rights advocates around the world have long been abolitionist in terms of the death penalty, often even using the term "abolition" as a shorthand for the elimination of capital punishment. The Council of Europe (2007: 2) correctly sees itself as "a pioneer for the abolition of capital punishment, considering it to be a grave violation of human rights," despite the ECHR's initial carving out of an exception for the death penalty in Article 2's right to life. In 1982, after a number of member states had abolished the death penalty, the Council adopted Protocol No. 6 to the Convention, which prohibited the death penalty during peacetime. In 1989, it made abolition of the death penalty in peacetime a condition of accession. In 2002, it adopted Protocol 13 requiring complete abolition of capital punishment. With the large majority of member states having ratified both protocols and all states observing at least a moratorium on capital punishment, the ECtHR ruled in 2010 that Article 2 had essentially been amended to prohibit the death penalty.[11]

For many, abolition of the death penalty would of course lose its power as an aspirational turning point for penal abolition if it were to lead to increased numbers of people in prisons, particularly with long sentences. That result has occurred in the United States, where sentences of life without parole (LWOP), often referred to as "irreducible life sentences" in Europe, have been on the rise for some years, partly as a result of the success of death penalty abolitionists in decreasing the number of death sentences being sought and handed down (Kleinstuber, Joy, and Mansley 2016: 186).[12] Europe has gone a different direction, apparently heeding Michel Foucault's observation, in reference to

---

[11] *Al-Saadoon and Mufdhi* v. *The United Kingdom*, App. No. 61498/08 (Eur. Ct. H.R. Apr. 10, 2010). Belarus, which is not a member of the Council of Europe, is the only European country that continues to apply the death penalty. The European Union has called for Belarus to abolish or at least put in place a formal moratorium on the use of capital punishment (European Union 2021: paras. 4–5).

[12] Even in states that have not abolished the death penalty, prosecutors increasingly seek LWOP, given how costly death penalty cases are to prosecute. Because defendants are often bargaining in the shadow of the death penalty, they are more likely to enter into plea agreements for

France's elimination of capital punishment in 1981, that death penalty abolition should not be the end game: "The real dividing line, among penal systems, is not between those that include the death penalty and the other ones; it divides those who admit permanent sentences and those that reject them" (Jouet 2022: 217, quoting Foucault 2001: 1025).

In contrast to the United States, relatively few countries in Europe had irreducible life sentences by the beginning of the twenty-first century. Where they continued to exist, the ECtHR limited their application over the years in a variety of cases (Szydło 2012: 626). Most importantly, in 2013 in *Vinter* v. *The United Kingdom*, the Court found irreducible life sentences to violate Article 3 of the Convention.[13]

Mugambi Jouet (2022: 212) sees the *Vinter* decision as one of two "promising developments in Europe" that he believes those who disparage mass incarceration, especially in the United States, should recognize for the guidance they might offer.[14] While acknowledging harsh sentencing and systemic racism in Europe, he lauds these developments, essentially treating them as what others might label non-reformist reforms. That is, he argues that, notwithstanding "his image as a nihilist" (204), Foucault would support them as promoting "anti-reformist activism" (Jouet 2022: 212, quoting Thibaud 1979: 4–5).[15]

Those who applaud the Court's treatment of irreducible life sentences, however, rarely take into account the Court's statement in *Vinter* that *reducible* life sentences (which are still permitted) merely require that domestic authorities "consider whether any changes in the life prisoner are so significant, and such progress towards rehabilitation has been made in the course of the sentence, as to mean that continued detention can no longer be justified on legitimate penological grounds."[16] The subsequent case of *Hutchinson* v. *The United Kingdom* (2017) granted the UK a wide margin of appreciation as to which and how domestic authorities might make that determination.[17]

LWOP. Importantly, in many states, defendants facing possible LWOP are not entitled to the same level of defense as are those facing the death penalty (Aspinwall 2021).

[13] *Vinter and Others* v. *The United Kingdom*, App. Nos. 66069/19, 130/10, and 3896/10 (Eur. Ct. H. R. Jul. 9, 2013) (Grand Chamber).

[14] The other development he discusses is the Council of Europe's passage of the European Prison Rules in 2006 (Jouet 2022: 3, 16). For a critique of these and related human rights–based prison rules for contributing to prison bureaucratization and thereby legitimating and extending penal control, see Armstrong 2018.

[15] For additional discussion of Foucault's penal abolitionism as well as some of his advocacy work regarding prisoners, see Charbit and Ricordeau 2021: 160–161; Vergès 2022: 66–67; Zurn and Dilts 2016.

[16] *Vinter and Others* v. *The United Kingdom* (Grand Chamber), para. 119.

[17] *Hutchinson* v. *The United Kingdom*, App. No. 57592/08 (Eur. Ct. H.R. Jan. 17, 2017) (Grand Chamber), para. 45.

Although some recent case law suggests that *Hutchinson* might be an outlier in terms of the margin of appreciation (Celiksoy 2020),[18] the ECtHR has come nowhere close to eliminating long sentences or even those that might in the end last a lifetime.[19] While, as I discuss in Section 2.2.3, some credit *Vinter* with the "right to hope," that right seems cruel for those who might have served many years, even decades, in prison, only to be evaluated periodically and have the authorities repeatedly determine that they are unfit to reenter society.[20] And it would certainly be a mistake to read the case law as anticipating anything close to abolition. Indeed, for Ailbhe O'Loughlin (2021: 538), "the Court's failure to challenge the assumptions underpinning life sentences risks further entrenching the trends of punitiveness and risk aversion it has tried to resist."

2.2.3 Rehabilitation

Many have read *Vinter* as reflecting a commitment by the Court to rehabilitation. For Jouet (2022: 217), for example, "*Vinter* reasoned that prisoners must not be reduced to their worst act and eliminated from society." Natasa Mavronicola (2014: 297) contends that the decision is "a clear rejection of purely retributive whole life sentences, based primarily on the penological principle of rehabilitation." She quotes the Court's statement that under an irreducible life sentence, a prisoner "can never atone for his offence: whatever the prisoner does in prison, however exceptional his progress towards rehabilitation, his punishment remains fixed and unreviewable."[21]

Relatedly, a number of scholars (Jouet 2022; Trotter 2022) have made much of the reference to a "right to hope" in Judge Power-Forde's concurring opinion in *Vinter*, and in a majority opinion in a subsequent case. Specifically, Judge Power-Forde wrote of those receiving irreducible life sentences: "Long and deserved though their prison sentences may be, [prisoners] retain the right to hope that, someday, they may have atoned for the wrongs which they have committed .... To deny them the experience of hope would be to deny a fundamental aspect of their humanity and, to do that, would be

---

[18] Even before the more recent judgments, Dirk van Zyl Smit and Catherine Appleton (2019: 57) concluded that "the survival of LWOP in Europe is somewhat precarious" with "a real possibility that all variations" will eventually "be regarded as contrary to fundamental human rights."
[19] For a recent statement of the Court's requirements and the extent to which domestic laws comply with them, see Department for the Execution of Judgments of the European Court of Human Rights 2023.
[20] States vary widely on their requirements for when and how often life sentences must be reviewed. The ECtHR has not articulated an acceptable timeline for review but has found that one conducted after twenty-five years of incarceration was sufficient. See O'Loughlin 2021. For a critique of politics and practices of hope in a different setting, see Parla 2019.
[21] *Vinter and Others* v. *The United Kingdom* (Grand Chamber), para. 112.

degrading."[22] These words were repeated four years later in *Matiošaitis and Others* v. *Lithuania*,[23] this time in a majority opinion. As Trotter (2022: 5) notes, these decisions marked the pivotal moment when "the idea of the 'right to hope' emerged in European Human Rights Law." For Jouet (2022: 216), "the right to hope" entails "a meaningful opportunity to reenter society based on one's rehabilitation."

While rehabilitation is sometimes seen as resonating with abolition, as at least a non-reformist reform in the way Jouet suggests, it could also be seen as conflicting with abolitionist aims. Using prisons for rehabilitation arguably adds to their legitimacy. Further, rehabilitation only addresses those who are already caught up in the criminal punishment system, and it assumes not only that they have committed the acts of which they are accused but that those acts should be criminalized. In other words, rehabilitation does not account for the possibility of improper conviction or the abolitionist contention that, as Thomas Ward Frampton (2022: 2034) puts it, "prison is rarely where we house those who are most responsible for inflicting the greatest harm on others."

Further, in practice, rehabilitation today often simply refers, as Sonja Meijer (2017: 150) explains, to "a state effort to prevent and neutralize the unwanted harmful side effects of incarceration," which means "that the rehabilitative activities should limit the detrimental effects of the detention itself."[24] In this telling, rehabilitation is aimed at reversing the harm caused by incarceration rather than preventing the harm to begin with.

Perhaps most importantly, the ECtHR does not in fact seem committed to rehabilitation as its overriding justification for punishment. As discussed in Section 4.2, the Court most often asserts deterrence as the rationale, even though it does little to demonstrate that the possibility of punishment deters human rights violations. Some see the Court as principally acting on a retributive rationale.

2.2.4 Prison Overcrowding and Detention as a Last Resort

Isobel Renzulli finds some glimpse of prison abolition in ECtHR rulings on prison overcrowding. That area is the only one, it seems, where the Court directly suggests alternatives to incarceration. Specifically, Renzulli (2022: 108) gives the example of judgments that "require a decrease in the reliance on the prison system through the adoption of alternative measures to

---

[22] *Vinter and Others* v. *The United Kingdom* (Grand Chamber) (Power-Forde, J., concurring), para. 54.
[23] *Matiošaitis and Others* v. *Lithuania*, App. Nos. 22662/13, 51059/13, 58823/13, 59692/13, 59700/13, 60115/13, 69425/13, and 72824/13 (Eur. Ct. H.R. May 23, 2017), para. 180.
[24] For the obligation to rehabilitate, Meijer (2017: 150) cites *Murray* v. *The Netherlands*, App. No. 10511/10 (Eur. Ct. H.R. Apr. 26, 2006) (Grand Chamber), para. 104.

incarceration and reducing use of pre-trial detention."²⁵ In at least one instance, she notes, the Court ruled that a state that cannot ensure that prison conditions are in accordance with Article 3 "must either abandon its strict penal policy or put in place a system of alternative means of punishment" (107).²⁶ Further, "[t]he court has also suggested reductionist types of measures, such as the use of shorter custodial sentences, replacing imprisonment with other forms of penalty, increasing the use of various forms of early release, and suspending the enforcement of some custodial sentences" (107).²⁷

Sonja Snacken (2022: 39) explains that these and additional decisions on prison overcrowding have been decided as pilot judgments. Pilot judgments provide a means of "identifying the structural problems underlying repetitive cases against many countries and imposing an obligation on States to address those problems" (European Court of Human Rights 2023: 1). The Court issues them in accordance with ECHR Article 46, which assigns the Committee of Ministers the duty to supervise the execution of judgments. In 2004, the Committee issued a resolution encouraging the Court to give states and the Committee guidance by identifying "underlying systemic or structural problems" (European Court of Human Rights 2024a, quoting Res. (2004) 3). The pilot judgments procedure provides one way in which the Court has both identified and responded to systemic issues.

In the specific judgments Snacken (2022) discusses, the Court identifies "that prison overcrowding results from structural problems relating to overly repressive penal policies," which the Court encourages states to address (39).²⁸ These judgments have in fact led several states to amend their penal codes to reduce the length of sentences and expand the possibilities for early release or community sanctions (Snacken 2022: 39, citing Cliquennois, Snacken, and van Zyl Smit 2021).

In addition, over the past twenty years the ECtHR has applied a strict proportionality test to assess whether pretrial detention violates Article 5 of the ECHR, stating that detention is "such a serious measure that it is justified only as a last resort" (Snacken 2022: 41, quoting and discussing *Saadi* v. *The*

---

[25] Citing *Torreggiani and Others* v. *Italy*, App. No. 43517/09 (Eur. Ct. H.R. Jan. 8, 2013), para. 69; *Varga and Others* v. *Hungary*, App. Nos. 14097/12, 45135/12, 73712/12, 34001/13, 44055/13, and 64586/13 (Eur. Ct. H.R. Mar. 10, 2015), para. 104.
[26] Citing *Orchowski* v. *Poland*, App. No. 17885/04 (Eur. Ct. H.R. Oct. 22, 2009), para. 153.
[27] Citing *Neshkov and Others* v. *Bulgaria*, App. Nos. 36925/10, 21487/12, 72893/12, 73196/12, 77718/12, and 9717/13 (Eur. Ct. H.R. Jan. 27, 2015), para. 276.
[28] In the pilot judgment in *Rezmives and Others* v. *Romania*, for instance, the Court acknowledged recommendations made by other European institutions, which Snacken notes include preventing overcrowding by decriminalizing certain offenses and fostering community-based measures (Snacken 2022, citing *Rezmives and Others* v. *Romania*, App. Nos. 61467/12, 39516/13, 48213/13, and 68191/13 [Eur. Ct. H.R. Apr. 25, 2017], para. 42).

United Kingdom[29]). Snacken argues that legal instruments of the Council of Europe, particularly by the CPT and Committee of Ministers, extend beyond pretrial detention. That is, they demonstrate "a large consensus on *always* using imprisonment as a last resort" and call for the promotion of alternative community sanctions (42). She faults the ECtHR for not applying its own approach to pre-trial detention or these instruments to its consideration of post-conviction sentencing, which it has "left almost exclusively to the national authorities" (41).

To the extent that the pilot judgments on prison overcrowding encourage states to reduce the prison population rather than build new carceral spaces, they might well suggest abolitionist resonances. The same might be said of the last resort approach to criminalization, especially were the Court to apply it beyond pretrial detention.

That said, penal minimalism, of which last resort is a principle, was originally coined as a term in the mid 1980s by Italian Luigi Ferrajoli to make clear his differences from both abolitionists and penal maximalists (Langer 2020: 54, citing Ferrajoli 2000: 126). While Máximo Langer (2020: 72) contends that there is an overlap in substantive commitments between abolitionists and at least Langer's own version of penal minimalism (such as a strong anti-subordination constitutional principle), others argue that maintaining criminal law even as a last resort leaves open the possibility for the legitimacy of criminalization and the "human rights violations [that] are, in practice, systematically committed in spaces of confinement" (Tapia Tapia 2024: 99).

2.3 Police Abolition and the Council of Europe

Parallel to some of its decisions involving prisoners' rights, the Court has in many instances identified police brutality as a violation of human rights, finding states responsible for excessive use of force by police in violation of Article 2 or 3 (Murdoch and Roche 2013: 25–42). It also has found violations of Article 5's prohibition on arbitrary deprivation of liberty when police have unlawfully detained or arrested individuals, subjected detainees to unwarranted or disproportional levels of compulsion and duress, or failed to inform detainees promptly of the reason for their detention (Murdoch and Roche 2013: 25–42). As we see in Section 3.1.2, the ECtHR has also deemed some of these actions to violate Article 14's prohibition on discrimination, given the enormous amount of policing that negatively affects the rights of racial, ethnic, religious, and sexual minorities.

---

[29] *Saadi v. The United Kingdom*, App. No. 13229/03 (Eur. Ct. H.R. Jan. 28, 2008) (Grand Chamber), para. 70.

Through these and other cases, the Court, implicitly at least, suggests a variety of changes that states need to make in relation to policing. In 2013, the Council of Europe used the case law, along with the work of the European Committee for the Prevention of Torture (CPT), to create a policing handbook (Murdoch and Roche 2013). The handbook is aimed at the "establishment of clear rules (in relation to the use of force)" to stop particular police practices. Importantly, it maintains that "[t]reatment in violation of European standards is by no means restricted to certain countries," referencing a report by the CPT finding that, in Switzerland, "'information gathered suggests that the phenomenon of police brutality witnessed by the CPT in the past' remained current" (23).

As much as the ECtHR has found certain police practices to constitute human rights violations in ways that resonate with or at least support the claims made by many police abolitionists, it has also justified a number of police practices. Some of these justifications can be found enshrined in the Council of Europe's policing handbook. In its consideration of Article 5, for example, the handbook cites several cases in which the Court found that there had been no violation (Murdoch and Roche 2013: 43–47). Further, the handbook makes clear that its goal is not to reduce but improve – and perhaps even expand – policing. Noting concern that ill-treatment by police has a negative effect on public support (113), one of the handbook's stated primary goals is to increase public trust in (and respect for) the police, largely through increased training and the development of greater professionalism (7, 8, 23, 106, 147). As discussed in Section 3.2, police abolitionists nearly always reject increased training for police as a reformist reform that, among other results, channels increased funding to police.

Setting the stage for the expansion of policing, the handbook rejects "that the notion of 'human rights' can be perceived of as a 'charter for the criminal'" (21). It identifies positive obligations stemming from a number of ECtHR decisions in the 1990s that require states to "undertake a criminal investigation, or to intervene in a situation where there is a real risk of domestic violence, or where there is an identifiable risk of violence from another person, or where the rights of protestors are under threat from counter-demonstrators" (15).[30] For the handbook, these cases requiring police intervention create "heightened responsibilities upon the police to protect victims from exploitation" and constitute "important developments in human rights jurisprudence" (21). Even scholars concerned about the broader ECtHR trend toward carceral, or coercive, human

---

[30] Citing, respectively, *Aydin* v. *Turkey*, App. No. 23178/94 (Eur. Ct. H.R. Sep. 25, 1997); *Opuz* v. *Turkey*, App. No. 33401/02 (Eur. Ct. H.R. Jun. 9, 2009); *Osman* v. *The United Kingdom*, App. No. 23452/94 (Eur. Ct. H.R. Oct. 28, 1998); *Plattform "Ärzte für das Leben"* v. *Austria*, App. No. 10126/82 (Eur. Ct. H.R. Jun. 21, 1988).

rights have largely missed the Court's imposition of these positive obligations regarding policing, which I return to in Section 3.2.

The resonances and dissonances I have discussed between human rights and both prison and police abolition highlight possibilities as well as pitfalls for relying on human rights law for abolitionist practice. In Section 3, I consider these and other dissonances as I read the Court's case law involving gendered and racialized violence. In Section 4, I return to some of the resonances for the ways they might help the Court become abolitionist-oriented.

3 Jurisprudence on Gendered and Racialized Violence

In this section, I explicitly bring prison and police abolitionist approaches to the ECtHR's coercive human rights case law. I do so through consideration of what many deem to be the hardest cases for critiquing the Court's invocation of positive obligations to investigate, prosecute, and punish: those involving racialized and gendered violence. Indeed, as I detail in this section and already suggested in the discussion of sex work, even some of those who are most critical of coercive human rights make exceptions for these types of cases, often on the grounds that the victims are vulnerable and in special need of attention. In fact, many call for *increased* criminal sanctions and policing.

Feminist, critical race, and queer abolitionists (and many at the intersection) have also long grappled with racialized and gendered violence but have come to a different conclusion: abolition provides a better vision than criminal punishment for preventing and responding to violence. Many European feminists, for example, aligned with abolitionists as early as the 1970s, with sexual and gender-based violence specifically in mind. In the United States, feminist abolitionists, many of color, worked within the abolitionist movement to insist that attending to gender-based violence is central to the larger structural changes needed to make abolition a reality. Further, queer abolitionists opposing homophobic and transphobic violence have explicitly opposed increased punishment for hate crimes. And many who fight against racist violence have used renewed public attention to police violence to focus on dismantling, rather than prosecuting, the police. Relatedly, many feminist and queer theorists and activists call for their movements to decrease their reliance on policing.

As with these abolitionists, I do not shy away from cases about domestic, sexual, racial, or transphobic or homophobic violence. To the contrary, I concentrate on these forms of violence – to emphasize that they are both harmful and quotidian and that they demand meaningful and effective responses. Rather than preventing this violence or addressing its structural causes, abolitionists contend, increased policing and criminal punishment often lead to even greater harm, including to some of the same groups they purportedly protect.

I follow the lead here of British criminologist Barbara Hudson (1998: 254) who, in an article entitled "Restorative Justice: The Challenge of Sexual and Racial Violence," stated: "What should be taken from feminist, anti-racist, and other 'zero tolerance' campaigners is that racial, sexual, and domestic violence should always be taken seriously." At the same time, she insisted, we should take from abolitionists "that punishment is morally problematic in that it involves the state inflicting pain or deprivation on an individual; that it deflects attention from the victim; that it generally offers little by way of protection and usually makes people worse rather than better" (254).

Partly as a result of advocacy organizations working on behalf of specific identity-based groups, a significant amount of ECtHR jurisprudence addresses racialized and gendered violence. In these cases, not only does the Court generally conclude that states have failed in their positive obligations to police, investigate, prosecute, or punish but it regularly finds that states should increase the length or intensity of punishment to respond adequately to the harm. The Court often justifies this inflated penal response, directly or indirectly, through its identification of the victims as vulnerable and the equation of vulnerability with increased harm.

As in human rights law and discourse more broadly, references to vulnerability are ubiquitous in the ECtHR's jurisprudence, with over 500 references to it in the merits of Article 3 cases alone (Heri 2020: 95). The Court has construed many groups and individuals as vulnerable, including children, victims of sexual and domestic violence, LGBT individuals, non-nationals, migrants, historically oppressed racial or ethnic minorities such as the Roma, and followers of minority religions.[31] Both implicitly and explicitly, assumptions of and about vulnerability feed many calls for criminal punishment (see, for example, Heri 2020: 97–111; Stavros 2020: 130–137; Zimmerman 2015: 554–559).

For then-Judge Tulkens (2012: 158), this connection between vulnerability and criminal punishment undermines a penal minimalist approach: "[T]he idea that criminal law must protect the fundamental rights of the weakest and most vulnerable" makes it difficult "not only to advance but especially to make it understood, in the Court, that criminal law does not necessarily constitute the only solution, that criminal intervention should remain, in theory and in practice, a final remedy."

Human rights advocates nevertheless often seek a recognition of vulnerability because they see it as a demonstration that the court is taking seriously particular – often gendered and racialized – harms. As Corina Heri (2020: 95) puts it, even

---

[31] For one discussion of the benefits and risks of being treated as a vulnerable group by the Court, see Peroni and Timmer 2013.

while expressing other concerns about the Court's vulnerability designation, vulnerability "'acts as a magnifying glass,' making ill-treatment ... look bigger."[32] In the context of the Article 3 cases she considers, it enables the Court more easily to find "that the threshold of severity has been met" (96). While Heri (2020: 116) is careful to acknowledge that a vulnerability designation "does not always automatically entail coercive obligations," it makes it more likely that the Court will impose positive obligations on a state to apply more or more stringent criminal law. For Stephanos Stavros (2020: 120), those groups that are considered (or he assumes are) vulnerable want criminal law "because of its symbolic value, the powerful message that it carries." Further, he contends, "[t]hey also consider it preferable – or even necessary – for practical reasons, as in this case the main resource-mobilisation burden is borne by the state."[33]

Heri's defense of the vulnerability designation and treatment is particularly striking because she is aware of and concerned more generally about coercive overreach. But she nevertheless sees the vulnerability approach as both providing "a more nuanced and targeted understanding of coercive positive obligations" and protecting "vulnerable applicants *from* coercive power" (Heri 2020: 115–116).

3.1 ECtHR Jurisprudence through a Prison Abolitionist Lens

In the remainder of this section, I explore and bring an abolitionist lens to some of the ECtHR's jurisprudence imposing positive obligations on states to criminalize certain acts against individuals from groups generally identified as vulnerable. I do so by focusing first on the Court's treatment of sexual and gender-based violence, before turning to some of its jurisprudence on violence against racial, ethnic, and sexual minorities that the Court finds to be hate-motivated or discriminatory. In many of these cases, the Court cites other human rights bodies in its analysis, demonstrating a widespread contemporary human rights common sense about the need for criminal punishment to address these harms.

3.1.1 Sexual and Gender-Based Violence

Some trace the obligation on states to use criminal law to the ECTHR's 1985 judgment in *X and Y v. The Netherlands*. There, the Court ruled that a father's inability under Dutch law to bring a criminal complaint against the suspected

---

[32] Heri attributes the magnifying glass concept that she quotes to Peroni and Timmer (Heri 2020: 1079).

[33] At the same time, Stavros (2020: 120) notes that others find the criminalization of hate speech to be "particularly objectionable, making reference to the very function of the criminal law and the need for restraint in terms of its mobilization."

rapist of his daughter with mental disabilities violated Article 8 of the ECHR. The Court recognized that "[r]ecourse to the criminal law is not the only answer,"[34] but found that the protection afforded by civil law was "insufficient" in that instance, "where fundamental values and essential aspects of private life are at stake."[35] The Court further observed that rape was an "area in which the Netherlands has generally opted for a system of protection based on the criminal law" but had simply omitted to extend it to these circumstances.[36]

The Court's specific articulation of positive obligations to prosecute and punish took nearly another twenty years. In its 2003 judgment in *M. C. v. Bulgaria*, a rape case involving a fourteen-year-old girl, the Court, relying in part on *X and Y*, unequivocally stated that states "have a positive obligation inherent in Articles 3 and 8 of the Convention to enact criminal-law provisions effectively punishing rape and to apply them in practice through effective investigation and prosecution."[37]

Today, after another twenty years, it is hard to imagine challenging that conclusion. But at the time, then-Judge Tulkens authored a concurring opinion indicating that, while "recourse to the criminal law may be understandable" in this type of case, in general "criminal proceedings should remain, both in theory and practice, a last resort."[38] She was particularly concerned that the Court had read *X and Y* too broadly, missing its important caveat that criminal law is "not the only answer."[39] Referencing the 1980 *Report on Decriminalisation* later discussed by Pinto, she stated that its observations "clearly show that the effectiveness of general deterrence based on the criminal law depends on various factors and that such an approach 'is not the only way of preventing undesirable behaviour.'"[40]

Notwithstanding Judge Tulkens' attempt to narrow the ruling in *M. C.*, the Court has continued to apply the positive obligations articulated there to cases involving what it identifies as serious human rights violations. Especially in cases involving sexual violence, the Court often pursues one of the rationales for the positive obligations that it set forth in *M.C.*, which is that "[c]hildren and other vulnerable individuals, in particular, are entitled to effective protection."[41] The Court does not require an explicit finding of vulnerability to support the broader obligation to punish but, as Heri (2020: 108) argues, "being considered

---

[34] *X and Y v. The Netherlands*, App. No. 8978/80 (Eur. Ct. H.R. Mar. 26, 1985), para. 24.

[35] *X and Y v. The Netherlands*, para. 27. For but one discussion of the historical significance of the case, see Mavronicola and Lavrysen 2020: 4–5.

[36] *X and Y v. The Netherlands*, para. 27.

[37] *M. C. v. Bulgaria*, App. No. 39272/98 (Eur. Ct. H.R. Dec. 4, 2003), para. 153.

[38] *M. C. v. Bulgaria* (Tulkens, J., concurring), para. 2.

[39] *M. C. v. Bulgaria* (Tulkens, J., concurring), para. 2.

[40] *M. C. v. Bulgaria* (Tulkens, J., concurring) (quoting European Committee on Crime Problems 1980: 75–78), para. 2.

[41] *M. C. v. Bulgaria*, para. 150.

vulnerable works in applicants' favor." Heri faults the Court for not expanding this analysis to clearly cover all adult victims (as opposed primarily to children or those with other intersecting vulnerabilities such as disability) (107–109).

Vulnerability plays a more central role in the ECtHR's recognition of states' positive obligations to investigate, prosecute, and punish domestic violence. In *Opuz* v. *Turkey* (2009), the ECtHR handed down a decision finding that the state's failure to take adequate criminal law measures to prevent domestic violence resulting in death constituted not only a violation of Articles 2 and 3 but also of Article 14's prohibition of discrimination.[42] In a judgment that human rights and women's rights advocates widely celebrated as landmark at the time, the Court also affirmed multiple regional and international findings and policies, including those of the CEDAW Committee, which oversees the implementation of the Convention on the Elimination of All Forms of Discrimination Against Women (CEDAW).[43] Vulnerability was key to the Court's decision. As Heri (2020: 108) notes, "[w]hile the Court does not consider women vulnerable as a group, it found in this case that the applicant was vulnerable, given the violence and threats she had suffered, her fear of further violence and her social situation as a woman in south-east Turkey."[44]

Later cases consider that victims of domestic violence are per se vulnerable, requiring state protection. In *Volodina* v. *Russia* in 2019, the Court explained: "The particular vulnerability of the victims of domestic violence and the need for active State involvement in their protection have been emphasised in a number of international instruments and the Court's case-law."[45] Vulnerability became one of the justifications for criminal sanctions in a later case involving the same applicant. There the Court made clear that civil proceedings would be insufficient, "reiterat[ing] that both the public interest and the interests of the protection of vulnerable victims from offences infringing on their physical or psychological integrity require the availability of a remedy enabling the perpetrator to be identified and brought to justice."[46] Only criminal law, it seems, could play this role.

---

[42] The first case to find that domestic violence could constitute a violation of the European Convention was *Kontrova* v. *Slovakia*, App. No. 7510/04 (Eur. Ct. H.R. May 31, 2007). That and a few subsequent decisions holding states accountable for domestic violence were decided under Article 2, Article 3, or Article 8, but none was decided under Article 14 before *Opuz*. For consideration of the use of different provisions over time, see McQuigg 2021b.

[43] For the Court's discussion of relevant work of the CEDAW Committee, see *Opuz* v. *Turkey*, paras. 72–77. For just some of the treatment of the case as landmark, see Abdel-Monem 2009; Buyse 2009; Council of Europe 2022; and Interights 2022.

[44] Heri cites *Opuz* v. *Turkey*, para. 160.

[45] *Volodina* v. *Russia*, App. No. 41261/17 (Eur. Ct. H.R. Jul. 9, 2019), para. 72 (citing previous case law).

[46] *Volodina* v. *Russia (no. 2)*, App. No. 40419/19 (Eur. Ct. H.R. Sep. 14, 2021), para. 57.

While in *Opuz* the Court considered that the law on the books – if properly applied – could have protected the victims,[47] in other cases it has found the legal framework wanting. In *Volodina*, for example, the Court found the state liable for violations of Article 3 and Article 14, pointing to the Russian law's failure to include domestic violence as either "a separate offence or an aggravating element of other offences."[48] Citing *Opuz* for the punishment requirement,[49] the Court concluded that the law fell short of "the State's positive obligation to establish and apply effectively a system punishing all forms of domestic violence and providing sufficient safeguards for victims."[50]

Two years later, in *Tunikova* v. *Russia*, the Court became more specific, noting that, notwithstanding *Volodina*, "in which the Court first identified structural defects of Russian law, the situation has not changed." It explained that "[l]egislation on domestic violence has not been passed or brought before Parliament. Public discussion on draft law on the prevention of domestic violence has not been followed with concrete action."[51] Focusing on these "structural defects," the Court used ECHR Article 46 to oblige Russia to change its domestic legal order, stating that "[d]omestic substantive law must criminalise and make punishable by appropriate penalties all acts of domestic violence," referencing again the need for the state to treat domestic violence as an aggravating factor or, to the same effect, a separate offense.[52] It then named a number of other substantive and procedural legal requirements.[53]

The Court's jurisprudence is aligned with the Council of Europe's Convention on Preventing and Combating Violence Against Women and Domestic Violence (Istanbul Convention). That convention, which entered into force in 2014 and has been ratified by thirty-eight member states (though not Russia), requires member states to ensure that domestic violence is considered as a possible aggravating factor in sentencing. Specifically, the Istanbul Convention's Article 46 listing aggravating factors includes that the violence was committed against a current or former intimate partner (46[a]) and that it was committed in front of a child (46[d]). Those provisions have been lauded by feminist legal scholars (for example, Leskinen 2020; Niemi and Sanmartin

---

[47] In particular, the Court stated that "the criminal-law system, as applied in the instant case, did not have an adequate deterrent effect capable of ensuring the effective prevention of the unlawful acts." *Opuz* v. *Turkey*, para. 153.
[48] *Volodina* v. *Russia*, para. 85.   [49] *Volodina* v. *Russia*, para. 85.
[50] *Volodina* v. *Russia*, para. 85.
[51] *Tunikova and Others* v. *Russia*, App. No. 55974/16, 53118/17, 27484/18, and 28011/19 (Eur. Ct. H.R. Dec. 14, 2021), para. 150.
[52] *Tunikova and Others* v. *Russia*, para. 154 (referencing para. 86). The Court further elaborates on both substantive and procedural criminal law requirements in the same paragraph as well as paras. 155–157.
[53] *Tunikova and Others* v. *Russia*, paras. 154–157.

2020), as has the ECtHR's jurisprudence on domestic violence more generally (for example, Kantack 2019; McQuigg 2021a; Petrova 2013). To the extent that the Court's jurisprudence has been criticized, it has been primarily for its failure on the ground to increase criminalization and prosecutions (for example, Gülel 2021; Human Rights Watch 2022a). As what many have labeled carceral feminism has taken hold,[54] it has become nearly common sense, including in human rights law and discourse, that states should be held accountable for not attending to gender-based violence with sufficiently harsh criminal punishment.

The near-agreement that human rights law should make states responsible for interpersonal violence is a significant achievement on the part of the women's human rights movement, which saw mainstream recognition for this position in the early 1990s.[55] Yet, the criminal punishment response to it, also supported by many women's human rights advocates, neglects historical and contemporary feminist abolitionist thought and activism, often rooted in anti-racist and anti-colonial struggles.[56] Again, abolitionist feminists take seriously the harms of violence against women but believe that, in general, penal responses only make things worse. They contend that finding meaningful alternative ways both to prevent and to respond to the violence should be central to any abolitionist project.

As part of her effort to outline a feminist decolonial perspective on violence, Françoise Vergès aims to combat historical amnesia about and revive insights from anti-carceral feminism in France. She details debates among the Women's Liberation Movement (MLF) in the 1970s about whether to appeal to the penal system to respond to acts of violence against women. Though those in the movement disagreed on some matters, she contends, nearly all refused the appeal to criminal law. They argued that such appeals would "admit the collective failure of the MLF, as repressive laws only 'reinforced and upheld rape and violence'" (Vergès 2022: 68, quoting from the June 25, 1976 edition of the movement journal *Le Quotidien des Femmes*). Relatedly, some argued against "pretending that respect for women will be measured in the number of years behind bars handed down in trials" (Vergès 2022: 69, quoting from an article in the French feminist magazine *Cahiers du Féminisme* 1980, no. 14). Well-known feminist lawyer and politician Gisèle Halimi contended that rape

---

[54] The identification and critique of carceral feminism can largely be traced to Elizabeth Bernstein, who has worked extensively on the issue for some time. Most recently, see Bernstein 2019. For a critique of carceral feminism in human rights in the context of sexual violence in conflict, see Engle 2020. For other contexts with a focus on the US, see Gruber 2020.

[55] For a genealogy of that transformation in thought within mainstream human rights, see Engle 2020: 28–44.

[56] For a discussion of the role of feminists in abolitionist movements in France from the 1970s, see Vergès 2022: 63–70.

sentences should be abolished or reduced. Importantly, she made clear that she was not calling for exceptional treatment of rape but was arguing within the context of opposition to long prison sentences in general (Vergès 2022: 69). Around the same time, Vergès recounts, a group of Italian feminists opposed an Italian law criminalizing violence against women that other feminists and the political left had promoted. In particular, the group eschewed the dependence upon the state that would require victims "to enter the courtroom to defend female dignity," calling instead for distance "from the law of the father which regulates sexuality and symbolization" (Vergès 2022: 70, quoting Librairie des femmes de Milan 2019: 116).

Vergès laments both the failure of an organized abolitionist feminist movement to emerge in France after the 1970s and the move toward carceralism that she dates to the 1980s. Her feminist decolonial approach pushes against that carceral turn, seeing "violence as a structural element of patriarchy and capitalism" and critiquing "the spontaneous recourse to the criminal justice system to protect so-called 'vulnerable' populations" (Vergès 2022: 4).

Notwithstanding the amnesia that Vergès identifies in France, many antiracist and anti-colonial feminists around the world have continued to make abolitionist arguments, including in relation to sexual and gender-based violence. Abolitionist feminists in the United States have been at the forefront of much of this thinking over the past two decades. Specifically, a group of women of color formed an organization in the late 1990s entitled INCITE! Women of Color Against Violence.[57] In 2001, they joined with abolitionist organization Critical Resistance to issue a joint Statement on Gender Violence and the Prison Industrial Complex, which addresses "both state AND interpersonal violence, particularly violence against women" (Critical Resistance and INCITE! [2001] 2008: 21).

The statement critiques mainstream carceral approaches to gender-related violence for fueling "the proliferation of prisons" and leading to increased imprisonment and deportation of women of color (Critical Resistance and INCITE! [2001] 2008: 22). At the same time, it calls on abolitionists to center gender and sexuality in their analysis and organizing, taking seriously the need to ensure safety and accountability for survivors of sexual and domestic violence. Concerned that many community-based alternatives "rely on a romanticized notion of communities, which have yet to demonstrate their commitment and ability to keep women and children safe or seriously address the sexism and homophobia that is deeply embedded within them" (23), the statement outlines

---

[57] The organization later changed its name to INCITE! Women, Gender Non-Conforming, and Trans People of Color Against Violence.

alternative analytics for developing community-based responses and action, including through the promotion of a holistic understanding of the roles of race, capitalism, colonialism, heterosexism, and patriarchy on both gender-based violence and the criminalization of poor communities (Critical Resistance and INCITE! [2001] 2008: 23–24).

In *Abolition. Feminism. Now.* (2022: 91), Davis, Dent, Meiners, and Richie situate INCITE! as foundational to the abolitionist feminism they promote, noting that INCITE!'s "influence as a *movement and a political identity* embodying a radical abolition feminism went far beyond its influence as an organization." This influence can be seen in the work of feminist abolitionists today in the United States as well as Europe (and elsewhere), in their responses to gender-based violence.

These ideas have also gained some traction among a broader group of feminist activists who have not always identified as abolitionist. Davis, Dent, Meiners, and Richie point to a 2020 open letter that garnered the signatures of forty-seven anti-violence coalitions across the United States. The letter self-critically notes the organizations' failure to attend to "Black feminist liberationists and other colleagues of color" who cautioned against a criminalization response to gender-based violence. In particular, the letter authors criticized their own attachment to "false solutions" based on reform, their refusal to heed that most survivors choose not to engage with the criminal legal system, and their failure to see the harm of prison while ignoring "transformative justice approaches to healing, accountability, and repair" (Davis et al. 2022: 77–78). Gaining traction is, of course, far from shifting the mainstream; a number of the signers, particularly those from mainstream shelters in conservative states, faced significant backlash for joining the letter (Davis et al. 2022: 78–79).

Another open letter galvanized a broad range of feminist groups in the United Kingdom, in their ultimately unsuccessful opposition to the 2022 Police, Crime, Sentencing and Courts Act. The letter opposed the bill in general, claiming that it would "adversely impact women, particularly racially minoritized women," and decried the parts of the bill that increased punishment for gender-based violence, which some members of Parliament had contended would increase women's safety (Working Chance 2021). With regard to the latter, the letter called on the bill's authors to "address the underlying causes of violence against women and girls," but through non-penal means, contending that "we urgently need a shift from the punitive approach championed by the Bill towards restorative and transformative justice that will actually make women safer" (Working Chance 2021). As British writer and activist Lola Olufemi (2021: 24) put it in her opposition to the criminalization embedded in the earlier Domestic Abuse Bill: "The most pressing issue[] for survivors is not that their abusers go to prison, but that there is a safety net for them to fall back on that enables them to leave abusive situations. They need refuges, routes to economic stability and adequate welfare support."

Bringing these abolitionist approaches to the advocacy and jurisprudence surrounding gender-based violence before the ECtHR would require a significant reorientation. Rather than finding states obligated to investigate, prosecute, and punish, advocates and the Court would heed the argument of a number of anti-carceral feminists, as summarized (if not fully endorsed) by Julie Goldscheid and Debra Liebowitz (2015: 313): "State criminalization and incarceration policies exacerbate and perpetuate interconnected forms of gender violence, particularly for racial, ethnic, religious, and sexual minorities, and for others from marginalized communities, such as indigenous, immigrant, and disabled survivors."[58]

3.1.2 Hate-Motivated Violence

The ECtHR also imposes positive obligations on states to ensure not only that crimes motivated by racism, homophobia, or transphobia are investigated, prosecuted, and punished but that perpetrators receive increased sentences as a result of the motivation. This jurisprudence is at times similar to that involving gender-based violence, particularly to the extent that the motive is seen as an aggravating circumstance.[59] And, as with the use of (and sometimes in combination with) the vulnerability designation, the Court and human rights advocates rely on increased punishment to express that the harm is particularly grave.

The cases about racist violence largely concern police violence, often against the Roma, with multiple claims having been brought against Bulgaria, Hungary, Italy, Romania, and Slovakia. According to "Uncovering Anti-Roma Discrimination in Criminal Justice Systems in Europe," a report by criminal legal system watchdog Fair Trials (2022: 6), "[d]iscriminatory and abusive police practices against Roma are widespread, often fuelled by negative stereotypes, and sometimes by outright hatred towards Roma." A European Roma Rights Centre (ERRC) study on racist policing against the Roma in the

---

[58] Goldscheid and Liebowitz (2015) cite, among others, Crago 2014: 367, 372–373; Davis 1985; Harris 2011; and Richie 2012. Leigh Goodmark expresses similar concerns about human rights law (Goodmark 2018: 115–116). She nevertheless argues for the United States to ratify CEDAW and take a human rights approach to domestic violence, with the claim that it would "lead to a more balanced policy response ... focused not just on the criminal system, but also on economic, cultural, and social rights" (Goodmark 2018: 141). For a later, more critical, argument that uses abolitionist thought to argue against disproportionate reliance on criminalization, though not in the context of international human rights, see Goodmark 2021: 13.

[59] For an argument that certain acts of gender-based violence should be treated as hate crimes, see Walters and Tumath 2014.

European Union (EU) (Rorke 2022: 6) similarly concludes that "racism is endemic and systemic within the ranks of officers paid to 'protect and serve,'" and "law enforcement agencies are saturated with institutional discrimination."

The Roma, of course, are not the only group to experience systemic racist police violence. A report commissioned by the European Parliament on the democratic oversight of policing (Guittet et al. 2022) recounts police violence throughout Europe against ethnic and racial minorities and migrants. It states succinctly: "Racism, discrimination, and police brutality are very much a European issue" (14). This violence is deeply rooted in colonialism. Vanessa E. Thompson (2021: 183) reminds us of Frantz Fanon's consideration of the role of policing in the colonies in his *The Wretched of the Earth*, where he identified police officers and soldiers as the "'official, instituted go-betweens' whose immediate presence and frequent and direct action towards colonised groups is characterised by everyday brute violence." And Didier Fassin (2019: 552) argues in his thick description of policing in France that "punitive policies and practices of law enforcement selectively oriented against ethnoracial minorities evoke the punitive law enforcement policies and practices toward colonial subjects."

The ECtHR's landmark case on racist police violence is *Nachova* v. *Bulgaria* (2005), in which the Court found that the state violated ECHR Article 2 combined with Article 14 for failing to investigate possible racial bias in the fatal shooting of two Roma individuals by the military police during an arrest. In language often repeated in subsequent cases, the Court emphasized that "[r]acial violence is a particular affront to human dignity," calling for "special vigilance and a vigorous reaction" and the use of "all available means to combat racism and racist violence."[60] In *Nachova* and subsequent judgments, the Court insisted that states must ensure that their laws distinguish between "racially induced violence and brutality" or, with regard to police violence, "cases of excessive use of force" and "[cases] of racist killing." Failing to do so is "to turn a blind eye to the specific nature of acts which are particularly destructive of fundamental rights."[61]

In *Nachova*, the Court viewed vigorous investigation as a way "to reassert continuously society's condemnation of racism and ethnic hatred."[62] Further, the

---

[60] *Nachova and Others* v. *Bulgaria*, App. Nos. 43577/98 and 43579/98 (Eur. Ct. H.R. Jul. 6, 2005) (Grand Chamber), para. 145. For similar language in other cases involving racially motivated police violence, see *Stoica* v. *Romania*, App. No. 42722/02 (Eur. Ct. H.R. Mar. 4, 2008), para. 117; *Lakatošová and Lakatoš* v. *Slovakia*, App. No. 655/16 (Eur. Ct. H.R. Dec. 11, 2018), para. 94; *R. R. & R. D.* v. *Slovakia*, App. No. 20649/18 (Eur. Ct. H.R. Sep. 1, 2020), para. 200.

[61] *Nachova and Others* v. *Bulgaria* (Grand Chamber), para. 160. See also *Stoica* v. *Romania*, para. 119; *Lakatošová and Lakatoš* v. *Slovakia*, para. 75; and *R. R. and R. D.* v. *Slovakia*, para. 201.

[62] *Nachova and Others* v. *Bulgaria* (Grand Chamber), para. 160.

Court asserted that such investigation will respond to the need "to maintain the confidence of minorities in the ability of the authorities to protect them from the threat of racist violence."[63] Distinguishing in both law and practice between racist and non-racist crimes will further help "maintain public confidence in [states'] law enforcement machinery."[64]

The ECtHR has followed a similar logic in considering police responses to violence committed by private actors. In a 2007 case against Croatia concerning an attack on a Roma individual by two members of a skinhead group, the Court stated that the need to distinguish between "racially induced violence and brutality" also applies to "cases where the treatment ... is inflicted by private individuals."[65] In the 2014 case of *Abdu* v. *Bulgaria*, the Court concluded that the state violated Article 3 in conjunction with Article 14 because the police investigation into a physical attack against two Sudanese nationals by two Bulgarian youths wearing Nazi insignia failed to consider possible racist motives.[66] Even though Bulgarian law makes racially motivated violence a separate crime and the police had access to evidence that the attack was racially motivated, the Court found, the police did not "take all reasonable measures to investigate a possible racist motive for the violence."[67]

The ECtHR is far from alone in this approach. Indeed, to bolster its reasoning, particularly in more recent cases, the Court has referenced the International Convention on the Elimination of All Forms of Racial Discrimination (ICERD) and the recommendations of the UN Committee on the Elimination of All Forms of Race Discrimination (CERD), which require penal responses to violence motivated by racial discrimination. In *Abdu*, for example, the Court approved of Bulgaria's enactment of the law criminalizing racist violence, noting that it "complied with the obligation flowing from [ICERD]."[68] Although it did not cite the provision, the Court was most certainly referencing Article 4 of the ICERD, which obliges states to "declare [as] an offence punishable by law ... all acts of violence or incitement to such acts against any race or group of persons of another colour or ethnic origin."[69] That provision, Patrick Thornberry (2016: 291) has noted, "appears to represent a kind of apotheosis of the punitive approach to addressing racial

---

[63] *Nachova and Others* v. *Bulgaria* (Grand Chamber), para. 160. See also *Lakatošová and Lakatoš* v. *Slovakia*, para. 96.
[64] *Nachova and Others* v. *Bulgaria* (Grand Chamber), para. 158. See also *Lakatošová and Lakatoš* v. *Slovakia*, para. 75.
[65] See *Šečić* v. *Croatia*, App. No. 40116/02 (Eur. Ct. H.R. May 31, 2007), paras. 66–67.
[66] *Abdu* v. *Bulgaria*, App. No. 26827/08 (Eur. Ct. H.R. Mar. 11, 2014).
[67] *Abdu* v. *Bulgaria*, paras. 49–50.   [68] *Abdu* v. *Bulgaria*, para. 47.
[69] International Convention on the Elimination of All Forms of Racial Discrimination Art. 4(a), Dec. 21, 1965, 660 UNTS 195.

discrimination." It is one of the few provisions in an early human rights treaty that arguably requires states to criminalize certain conduct.[70]

In other cases, the ECtHR has quoted relevant concluding observations by CERD. In a case against Slovakia involving an off-duty police officer shooting and killing several members of a Roma family, for instance, the Court quoted CERD concluding observations on Slovakia calling for the prosecution of hate crimes. The most recent one had specifically recommended that "all racially motivated crimes, including verbal and physical attacks, are investigated, that perpetrators are prosecuted and punished, and that motives based on race or on skin colour, descent or national or ethnic origin are considered as an aggravating circumstance when imposing punishment for a crime."[71] In the case at hand, the prosecutors had not treated racial motivation as a possible aggravating circumstance and, indeed, had "insufficiently investigated the racist aspects of the acts of violence."[72]

The ECtHR has followed a similar approach toward crimes with possible homophobic or transphobic intent, often citing the race cases, and holding that "violence and brutality with discriminatory intent" must be treated differently from "cases that have no such overtones."[73] Most of these cases find that the state failed in its positive obligation to use its police powers to protect individuals from hate crimes or to investigate adequately the crimes once they were reported. Some, including some of those same cases, also find the state responsible for discriminatory ill-treatment by police.[74]

---

[70] For a discussion of the other two early treaties with similar language, see Pinto 2018: 175 (citing Convention on the Prevention and Punishment of the Crime of Genocide, Jan. 12, 1951, 78 UNTS 77; Convention Against Torture and Other Cruel, Inhuman or Degrading Treatment or Punishment, Dec. 10, 1984, 1465 UNTS 85).

[71] *Lakatošová and Lakatoš* v. *Slovakia*, paras. 63–64.

[72] *Lakatošová and Lakatoš* v. *Slovakia,* para. 68; see also *R. R and R. D.* v. *Slovakia*, para. 123.

[73] *Identoba and Others* v. *Georgia*, App. No. 73235/12 (Eur. Ct. H.R. May 12, 2015), para. 67. For nearly identical language in other cases, see *Aghdgomelashvili and Japaridze* v. *Georgia*, App. No. 7224/11 (Eur. Ct. H.R. Oct. 8, 2020), para. 44; *Association Accept and Others* v. *Romania*, App. No. 19237/16 (Eur. Ct. H.R. Jun. 1, 2021), para. 124; *M. C. and A. C.* v. *Romania*, App. No. 12060/12 (Eur. Ct. H.R. Apr. 12, 2016), para. 124; *Oganezova* v. *Armenia*, App. Nos. 71367/12 and 72961/12 (Eur. Ct. H.R. May 17, 2022), para. 86; *Sabalić* v. *Croatia*, App. No. 50231/13 (Eur. Ct. H.R. Jan. 14, 2021), para. 94; *Women's Initiatives Supporting Group and Others* v. *Georgia*, App. Nos. 73204/13 and 74959/13 (Eur. Ct. H.R. Dec. 16, 2021), para. 63.

[74] See, for example, *Aghdgomelashvili and Japaridze* v. *Georgia*, paras. 44, 49–50. In a case against Russia that is largely about police failure to protect LGBT protesters, the Court also found that the state violated Article 11's freedom of assembly because of the police arrest of one of the protesters, though it fell short of finding discriminatory motive. *Berkman* v. *Russia*, App. No. 46712/15 (Eur. Ct. H.R. Dec. 1, 2020), paras. 59–63. Similar facts were present in the earlier case of *Identoba* as well, though the Court found that the applicants who stated that they had been improperly detained had not made that a part of their domestic complaints. *Identoba and Others* v. *Georgia*, para. 104.

Toward an Abolitionist Human Rights Court 33

The ECtHR emphasizes in nearly all these decisions that a homophobic or transphobic motivation should be legally treated as an aggravating factor for violent crimes. In many instances, domestic criminal law already provides for homophobic violence to constitute an aggravating factor, allowing the ECtHR to find that a criminal investigation or prosecution was not conducted in accordance with domestic law. In *Identoba and Others v. Georgia*, the first of the cases involving homophobic hate crimes, the Court referenced Georgia's criminal law that makes discrimination based on sexual orientation or gender identity an aggravating circumstance. It then stated that it is "essential for the relevant domestic authorities" to take "all reasonable steps with the aim of unmasking the role of possible homophobic motives."[75] It followed similar reasoning in a subsequent case against Georgia as well as in cases against Croatia and Romania.[76]

The Court has not limited its reasoning to those states that already make homophobic or transphobic motive an aggravating factor in their criminal codes. It reached a similar conclusion, for example, in cases against Armenia (*Oganezova v. Armenia*) and Bulgaria (*Stoyanova v. Bulgaria*), even though the criminal code of neither country made homophobic motive an aggravating element. While denying the applicants' request in both cases to require the state to amend its criminal code, insisting that the particularities of compliance should be left to the states, the Court made clear in *Oganezova* that "[d]iscriminatory remarks and insults must in any event be considered as an aggravating factor."[77] It also reiterated its own case law mandating "an effective application of domestic criminal-law mechanisms capable of elucidating the hate motive" and pointed to the state's failure to follow earlier recommendations by both the European Commission Against Racism and Intolerance (ECRI) and the UN Human Rights Committee.[78]

In *Stoyanova*, the Court invoked ECHR Article 46 to find that the violation was "of a systemic character" because it was embedded in law and then "to give some indications of how breaches of this kind are to be avoided in the future."[79] The Court made clear that Bulgaria should make the necessary legal changes (either through its code or the interpretation of it) to "ensure that violent attacks ... motivated by hostility towards the victim's actual or presumed

---

[75] *Identoba and Others v. Georgia*, para. 77.
[76] See *Association Accept and Others v. Romania*, para. 52; *Sabalić v. Croatia*, para. 102; *Women's Initiatives Supporting Group and Others v. Georgia*, para. 59.
[77] *Oganezova v. Armenia*, para. 81.
[78] *Oganezova v. Armenia*, paras. 103–104.
[79] *Stoyanova v. Bulgaria*, App. No. 56070/18 (Eur. Ct. H.R. Jun. 14, 2022), para. 78.

sexual orientation are in some way treated as aggravated in criminal law terms."[80]

LGBT human rights advocates have supported, if not encouraged, these rulings that require increased punishment for hate crimes. Some of the ECtHR's decisions expressly reference interventions in the case or reports by activists and advocacy organizations, demonstrating that this view has become common sense within LGBT human rights advocacy. For instance, in *Sabalić v. Croatia*, the ECtHR found a sentence that had resulted from a prosecution to be too lenient, "manifestly disproportionate to the gravity of the ill-treatment suffered by the applicant," because the prosecution did not take into account "a hate crime element as an aggravating factor for the offences involving violence."[81] The Court referenced the third-party intervention by the International Lesbian, Gay, Bisexual, Trans and Intersex Association of Europe (ILGA-Europe), which had claimed that "the most effective method" of implementing legislation against hate crimes is to create "enhanced penalties for all or specified crimes committed on the basis of a relevant bias." Alternatively, ILGA-Europe argued, the legislation could make motivation an aggravating factor.[82]

In its submission in the same case, Zagreb Pride pointed to the "institutionalised and social violence against LGBT persons in Croatia," who were "pushed to the margins of social life and faced with growing concerns over the rising number of violent attacks against them."[83] The organization simply assumed that harsher sentences would constitute an effective response to that structural violence. After the decision, the head of ILGA-Europe praised the Court for "send[ing] a strong signal to ... member states to ensure effective investigation, prosecution and punishment of homophobic and transphobic violent crimes" (ILGA-Europe 2021).

Bulgarian LGBT advocacy organization Deystvie intervened in *Stoyanova*, arguing, according to the Court, that "a particular problem arose from the lack of statutory provisions treating offenses motivated by hostility toward LGBTI people as 'aggravated' ones."[84] Once the case was decided, the organization worked successfully to help achieve a change in domestic law to ensure increased punishment for hate crimes. Several months later, its website's main

---

[80] *Stoyanova* v. *Bulgaria*, para. 79.
[81] *Sabalić* v. *Croatia*, paras. 110, 102, respectively. The Court's finding of a "manifestly disproportionate" sentence relies on a concept that, outside of the ECtHR, has generally been used to protect the human rights of defendants not to be punished too harshly. For discussion of other ECtHR cases that use the concept to refer to sentences that are too lenient, see Lavrysen 2020: 48; Mavronicola 2020: 186.
[82] *Sabalić* v. *Croatia*, para. 88. [83] *Sabalić* v. *Croatia*, para. 87.
[84] *Stoyanova* v. *Bulgaria*, para. 61.

page continued to feature a statement: "Victory for LGBTI+ people in Bulgaria: The Criminal Code adopted more severe penalties for crimes related to sexual orientation."[85]

Suggesting near agreement in human rights law and advocacy, the Court in *Sabalić* also cited a 2015 joint statement from twelve UN bodies, which called for "[i]ncorporating homophobia and transphobia as aggravating factors in laws against hate crime and hate speech."[86] Note the inclusion of hate speech. While most of the cases involving hate crimes include acts of physical violence, the ECtHR has inched close to criminalizing hate speech in both the race and LGBT contexts, favorably referencing the ICERD as well as ECRI recommendations.[87] It has done so notwithstanding the ECHR's Article 10 on the right to freedom of expression.

Stavros (2020: 124) praises this ECtHR case law, in which he contends that "the Court seems to have opted for a bolder stance," not only by permitting but sometimes by requiring states to criminalize hate speech. In the line of cases about groups he considers vulnerable, the Court has found that state response (or lack of response) to anti-Roma or anti-Muslim (or both) hate speech violates Article 8's right to private life or Article 9's right to religious freedom, sometimes in conjunction with Article 14 (Stavros 2020: 124–125).[88] The facts that gave rise to some of the violations in these cases also include physical violence, but Stavros reads the cases as not requiring it.

Similar reasoning on hate speech can be seen in several of the LGBT cases, particularly in those in which not all applicants suffered grave physical injuries. In *Identoba*, for example, the Court found "that the question of whether or not some of the applicants sustained physical injuries of certain gravity became less relevant" in light of the fact that all the applicants were "the target of hate speech and aggressive behaviour."[89] While the Court stated in *Association Accept and Others v. Romania* that it is "careful not to hold that each and every utterance of hate speech must, as such, attract criminal prosecution and criminal sanctions,"[90] it also reiterated its earlier holdings "that where acts that constitute serious offenses are directed against a person's physical or mental integrity, only efficient criminal law mechanisms can ensure adequate protection."[91]

---

[85] For its summary of the law, see Deystvie 2023. [86] *Sabalić v. Croatia*, para. 50.
[87] For discussion of much of the case law relying on these instruments, particularly in the context of racist hate speech, see Stavros 2020: 124–137.
[88] Stavros (2020: 124–125) cites *Alković v. Montenegro*, App. No. 66895/10 (Eur. Ct. H.R. Dec. 5, 2017); *Király and Dömötör v. Hungary*, App. No. 10851/13 (Eur. Ct. H.R. Jan. 17, 2017); and *R. B. v. Hungary*, App. No. 64602/12 (Eur. Ct. H.R. Apr. 12, 2016).
[89] *Identoba and Others v. Georgia*, para. 77.
[90] *Association Accept and Others v. Romania*, para. 119.
[91] *Association Accept and Others v. Romania*, para. 102.

Referencing multiple times the effect of the speech on the applicants' dignity, the Court found that the state's failure to protect applicants from and later investigate homophobic speech violated Article 8 combined with Article 14.

The decision in *Association Accept and Others* is arguably ambiguous about whether the state would have a positive obligation to criminalize this particular conduct, especially given the lack of physical harm. Two judges, however, were concerned enough about a reading that would require criminalization of hate speech that they authored a partly dissenting opinion emphasizing the ECtHR case law on using criminal law only as a last resort: "[T]he Court has acknowledged that criminal sanctions, including against the individuals responsible for the most serious expressions of hatred, inciting others to violence, could be invoked only as an *ultima ratio* measure."[92]

In contrast to these judges, human rights advocates today rarely invoke the concept of criminal law as a last resort, and generally see the criminalization of hate motivation as progressive. While the ECtHR's identification of likely racist and homophobic motivations behind otherwise "ordinary" acts of violence and brutality – by state and non-state actors alike – might lead to a better understanding of structural subordination, an abolitionist approach to human rights would reject using criminal punishment as the means for either calling attention to the severity of the harm or shifting structural power. And it would directly challenge the assumption that vulnerable or subordinated groups subjected to hate-motivated violence are in special need of the criminal punishment system. It would do so from the perspectives of many of those most directly harmed by both the violence and the carceral approach to it.

In the United States, where important actors in the civil rights movement have long sought criminal penalties in response to White supremacist violence, many activists today have begun to question the emphasis on criminally prosecuting police officers for their racist violence (Sinnar 2022: 562–563). As Kate Levine argues (2021: 1033), the idea

> that we can prosecute our way out of this violence leads us into the same fallacy that insists we rely on the police and on prison to be safe in the first place. Those who wish to stem this cycle must face the fact that prosecuting individual police officers both legitimizes the criminal legal system and further clouds the causes of police violence.

---

[92] *Association Accept and Others* v. *Romania* (Grozev, J. and Harutyunyan, J., partly dissenting), para. 9. A conservative Polish nongovernmental organization (NGO), Ordo Juris Institute for Legal Culture, argued that even Article 3 violations did not require a criminal response, an issue that was not addressed as the Court did not find a violation of Article 3. *Association Accept and Others* v. *Romania*, para. 51.

For Allegra McLeod (2019: 1639–1640), criminal prosecutions for racist police violence, by treating the violence as aberrational and excessive, "may even stand to legitimize policing practices in general, though those practices tend to dehumanize men, women, and children on a daily basis." Further, prosecutions "do not offer tangible recompense to survivors and others who have been harmed" (1640).

Some have aimed to build on the 2015 victory of the families of Black victims of torture by Chicago police between 1972 and 1991. Even though the police chief during those years was ultimately convicted of perjury and obstruction of justice (the statute of limitations had run for individual civil and criminal claims for the acts of torture), abolitionists insist that "the most important victory" (Davis et. al. 2022: 142) was the Chicago City Council's unanimous passage of an ordinance with an alternative response, specifically a reparations package (141–142). The package includes a $5.5 million fund; free college tuition, job training, and various forms of counseling for victims and their family members; an apology; a permanent memorial; and teaching of the case in the school curriculum (Ritchie et al. 2022). The set of reparations has been identified as a model by a number of abolitionists (for example, McLeod 2019: 1627; Roberts 2019: 117), including the Movement for Black Lives (Ritchie et al. 2022). For Joey Mogul (2015), who represented the victims and originally drafted the ordinance, "Chicago's approach to systemic racial harm offers a glimmer of a possible future in which the nation as a whole might finally grapple with reparations for the legacy of slavery, Jim Crow, and its direct descendant, mass incarceration."

Queer and anti-racist abolitionists have for years opposed hate crimes legislation, with queer abolitionists arguably taking the lead (for example, Lamble 2011: 243–246; Sinnar and Colgan 2020; Stanley, Spade, and Queer (In)Justice 2012: 126–127). The UK-based queer abolitionist scholar and activist Sarah Lamble summarizes the concerns well: "The problem with hate crime legislation is that it offers a false promise. It takes the symbolic aspect of recognising harm and channels it into a punitive response (tougher sentencing) that does little to stop violence and instead shores up the powers of the carceral state" (Lamble 2021: 125).

Queer abolitionists also often implore LGBTQ organizations that advocate for hate crimes legislation to attend to the consequences of increased criminalization on people of color, especially but not only queer and trans people of color. Lamble (2011: 125), for instance, calls out the "many LGBT organizations in Canada, Britain, and the United States – particularly white-dominated and class-privileged ones – [who] are increasingly complicit in the forces of prison expansion." Lamble points specifically to their "calling for increased penalties under hate crimes laws" as well as their "contributing to gentrification of poor, working-class and immigrant neighborhoods; and supporting 'quality of life' ordinances that drive queer and trans street youth from public spaces." Concluding a piece titled "Queer Abolitionist Alternatives to Criminalising Hate Violence," S. M. Rodriguez (2021) makes clear that "opposition to hate crimes legislation and discourse does not mean that we do not acknowledge the heightened threat of harm in our lives or to our queer bodies" but "that we duly acknowledge the *unparalleled* harm of the justice system to our Black/Brown and queer bodies, minds and hearts" (199).

Just as human rights advocates who favor the criminalization of hate motivation are often aligned across issues and movements, so too are abolitionists. Both sets of solidarities – and a clash between them – became apparent when, in response to the alarmingly dramatic increase in anti-Asian violence in the United States at the beginning of COVID-19, the US Congress considered federal legislation to monitor and use law enforcement to respond to hate crimes. After the Senate passed its version of the bill (but before the House had voted), over 100 Asian and LGBTQ, particularly trans, organizations came together to oppose it (Reappropriate 2021). "While we wish we could celebrate the historic visibility of anti-Asian violence and racism, which is as old as the colonization of the Americas," they explained, the bill "contradicts Asian solidarity with Black, Brown, undocumented, trans, low-income, sex worker, and other marginalized communities whose liberation is bound together." Increased law enforcement and criminalization, they insisted, "harms and furthers violence against Asian communities facing some of the greatest disparities and attacks – sex workers, low wage workers, people with disabilities, people living with HIV, youth, women, trans and non-binary people, migrants amongst others" – and "ignores that police violence is also anti-Asian violence, which has disproportionately targeted Black and Brown Asians."

Notwithstanding this opposition, the bill overwhelmingly passed both chambers and was enacted into law in May 2021.[93] It was presented and lauded as a human rights victory, including by the CERD in its concluding observations on the United States' periodic report to the committee in 2022. Though the concluding observations contained significant criticism of the US government, the CERD listed the legislation as one of seven "positive aspects" of the US human rights record (UN CERD 2022: para. 3). The UN's press release for the CERD's findings began its headline: "Experts of the Committee on the Elimination of Racial Discrimination Commend the United States of America

---

[93] COVID-19 Hate Crimes Act, Pub. L. No. 117–13, 135 Stat. 265 (2021).

on the COVID-19 Hate Crimes Act" (Office of the High Commissioner for Human Rights [OHCHR] 2022).

To the extent that the CERD was critical of the legislation, it faulted the law for the opposite of the concerns expressed by activists who opposed it. During the hearing, for instance, one committee member asked the delegation, according to the press release, to "explain why only a fraction of cases reported as hate crimes were qualified as such by the police and the decline in federal prosecution of hate crimes" (OHCHR 2022). Further, the CERD's concluding observations (UN CERD 2022: paras. 14–15) recommended that the United States make greater efforts to prohibit hate speech and, relatedly, lift its ongoing reservation to Article 4 of the ICERD.

An abolitionist-oriented ECtHR would not follow the CERD down the criminalization path. As I outline in Section 4, far from denying the harm of hate-based violence, it would bring a magnifying glass to the multilayered oppression experienced by subordinated groups that is both represented by and leads to carceral responses. It would stop calling for punishment and policing in these and other cases and might well hold states accountable, in a traditional negative rights sense, for the very ways that criminalization exacerbates and perpetuates racialized and gendered violence. It might then impose positive obligations on states to attend to the structural causes of hate-based violence and to repair the harm caused by it.

3.2 ECtHR Jurisprudence through a Police Abolitionist Lens

A number of the ECtHR's decisions, including a few that I have already discussed in Section 3.1, fault the police for inaction or insufficient action, especially in the case of those from groups that the Court sees as marginal or vulnerable. This *lack* of police action sits in tension with the many cases the Court hears in which the police have *overacted* (or simply acted), including against many of the same groups. Here, I unpack that tension through analysis of some of the Court's decisions that, by finding that states have failed in their obligations to provide adequate police protection, essentially place positive obligations on states to increase their police presence. I do so through a police abolitionist lens.

Although penal abolitionists have long envisioned a world without policing, specific movements have emerged in recent years focused on abolishing policing as we know it. These movements are largely in response to the types of police violence discussed in Section 3.1.2. Those who aim to abolish policing call for resources that currently go to the police to be redistributed to sites that will better respond to many of the issues that policing fails to address or even exacerbates – from security to poverty. Such radical redistribution might well go beyond what any court can do, especially on its own. Yet, the ECtHR could be guided by the insights of police abolitionists, not only as it responds to police violence but by not seeing policing as the best or even the proper response to other human rights violations.

At a general level, one could argue that decisions requiring that states investigate, prosecute, and punish perpetrators necessarily call for more policing, in ways that the policing handbook discussed in Section 2.3 anticipated. I have contended elsewhere, in the context of international pressure on Mexico to investigate what some termed "femicide" in Ciudad Juárez, that arrest, detention, and sometimes even torture of alleged perpetrators can provide an expedient way for states to indicate that they are responding to human rights violations by non-state actors (Engle 2015: 1125). Mattia Pinto (2020) and Liora Lazarus (2020) similarly consider the pressure that the ECtHR's jurisprudence has put on police to act preemptively, including in the context of the UK's Modern Slavery Act. Pinto (2020) explains that the ECtHR's "insistence on effective criminal enforcement motivates policing and prosecutorial responses rather than efforts to understand and deal with situations of systemic injustice" (180).

Of course, increased policing is rarely neutral. The UK and Ireland-based group Abolitionist Futures (2020) opposes hate crimes legislation in part because of its impact on policing, stating that it "is often used by police against communities of colour who already bear the brunt of policing." Further, the group contends, hate crimes legislation "entangles voluntary sector/community groups into working with police and diverts resources away from preventative measures" (Abolitionist Futures 2020).

If the ECtHR jurisprudence we have examined up to now implicitly calls for more policing, here I identify decisions that explicitly find that states have positive obligations to provide better or more policing in particular situations. Specifically, I consider the imposition of these positive obligations in two types of cases: those involving domestic violence and those addressing violence directed at LGBT demonstrators. These cases, though relatively few, are worth examining because they raise the question whether anyone, particularly those from subordinated, vulnerable, or over-criminalized groups, should rely on police to begin with. Police abolitionists have tackled this question head-on, as have others who have expressed concerned that police presence often exacerbates tense situations.

In the domestic violence cases I identify, the Court has condemned what it references as the "passivity" of the police, which generally means the failure of the police to arrest an alleged perpetrator or even criminally investigate claims of domestic violence.⁹⁴ In its 2021 judgment in *A. and B.* v. *Georgia*, for instance, the Court followed a long line of cases to conclude that the case was "yet another vivid example of how general and discriminatory passivity of the law-enforcement authorities in the face of allegations of domestic violence can create a climate conducive to a further proliferation of violence committed against victims merely because they are women."⁹⁵ Importantly, the Court suggested that more active policing would deter domestic violence, notwithstanding that "the abuser was himself a police officer,"⁹⁶ a matter I return to later in this section.

In the LGBT context, the ECtHR has called explicitly for more and better-funded policing. Two cases against Georgia are illustrative, both involving counter-protest harassment and violence during marches on the International Day Against Homophobia (IDAHOT), first in 2012 and then in 2013.⁹⁷ In *Identoba*, the first case in which the court articulated the need to treat homophobic and transphobic violence differently from violence without such motives, the Court faulted the police force both for its negative treatment of LGBT marchers and for its inaction. In terms of negative treatment, police officers arrested and removed some of the demonstrators from the scene, ostensibly to protect them from counter-demonstrators.⁹⁸ As for inaction, the Court referenced the "State's positive obligation to provide the peaceful demonstrators with heightened protection from attacks by private individuals," before noting that the "limited number of police patrol officers ... distanced themselves without any prior warning from the scene ... thus allowing the tension to degenerate into physical violence."⁹⁹

To fulfill its positive obligation, the Court suggested, the state would have needed to increase the number of police dispatched to the demonstration. Never indicating that the police who were present "distanced themselves" out of lack of human power or equipment, the Court nevertheless stated that "it would have been only prudent if the domestic authorities ... had ensured more police manpower by mobilizing, for instance, a squad of anti-riot police."¹⁰⁰ The

---

⁹⁴ The cases about police passivity often cite *Opuz* v. *Turkey*, though it addressed "judicial passivity." See, for example, *Bălșan* v. *Romania*, App. No. 49645/09 (Eur. Ct. H.R. May 23, 2017); *Talpis* v. *Italy*, App. No. 41237/14 (Eur. Ct. H.R. Mar. 2, 2021); *Tkhelidze* v. *Georgia*, App. No. 33056/17 (Eur. Ct. H.R. Jul. 8, 2021).

⁹⁵ *A and B* v. *Georgia*, App. No. 73795/16 (Eur. Ct. H.R. Feb. 10, 2022), para. 49.

⁹⁶ *A and B* v. *Georgia*, para. 48.

⁹⁷ Created in 2004, the International Day Against Homophobia, Transphobia and Biphobia (which goes by a variety of acronyms) is held on May 17, the date in 1990 on which the World Health Organization declassified homosexuality as a mental illness. The marchers intentionally chose this day to march rather than to hold a Gay Pride parade. *Identoba* v. *Georgia*, para. 12.

⁹⁸ *Identoba* v. *Georgia*, paras. 16–17.   ⁹⁹ *Identoba* v. *Georgia*, para. 73.

¹⁰⁰ *Identoba* v. *Georgia*, para. 99; see also *Berkman* v. *Russia*, paras. 51–58.

Court assumed, of course, that those police officers would use their power and weapons in a way that would protect the LGBT demonstrators.

At the following year's demonstration, counter-protests again took place. This time, with plenty of advanced notice, the Ministry of the Interior had deployed 2,000 police officers to cordon off the demonstrators from the counter-demonstrators. Yet, harassment and violence ensued, in part because counter-demonstrators breached the cordon. When a complaint in that case was brought to the ECtHR (*Women's Initiatives Supporting Group* v. *Georgia*), the Court found the state liable under both Article 3 and Article 11 (freedom of assembly), combined with Article 14, for failing to meet its positive obligation to protect the demonstrators. It cited the "passivity" of the police, including while the counter-demonstrators started to break the cordon.[101] But at the same time it found it "established beyond a reasonable doubt that the police in some places opened up the cordon for the counter-demonstrators."[102] Given this latter finding of direct police complicity in the violence, it is particularly striking that the Court faulted the state for deploying "unarmed and unprotected police patrol officers" – that is, for not "equipping law-enforcement officers deployed to the scene with appropriate riot gear in order to be able to discharge their police functions."[103] Of course, arms and riot gear in those circumstances would likely have made the situation worse. And one can imagine the police using the case to call for greater funding from the state, a definite anti-abolitionist move, as I discuss later in this section.

The Court also stressed that the demonstration's organizers had "specifically requested the police to provide protection against foreseeable protests by people with homophobic and transphobic views."[104] That the protection had been promised to them added to the harm: "The applicants' emotional distress must have been further exacerbated by the fact that the police protection which had been promised to them in advance ... was not provided in due time or adequately."[105]

Given the history of anti-LGBT violence not only in Georgia but in nearly every part of the world, the Court's suggestion that LGBT marchers would have expected the police to protect them seems a bit naïve. Indeed, by the time the

---

[101] *Women's Initiatives Supporting Group* v. *Georgia*, paras. 75–76. For a similar approach, see *Berkman* v. *Russia*, paras. 51–58 (finding that "passive" police conduct during the initial stage of a Coming Out Day event in St. Petersburg – namely, the failure of the police to stop homophobic verbal attacks and physical pressure by counter-demonstrators – amounted to noncompliance with the state's positive obligations; in *Berkman*, however, the Court noted that the police officers "outnumbered counter-demonstrators several times").

[102] *Women's Initiatives Supporting Group* v. *Georgia*, para. 75.

[103] *Women's Initiatives Supporting Group* v. *Georgia*, para. 73.

[104] *Women's Initiatives Supporting Group* v. *Georgia*, para. 72.

[105] *Women's Initiatives Supporting Group* v. *Georgia*, para. 60.

case was decided in 2022, police raids of a queer-friendly nightclub had contributed to the decision by NGOs to cancel IDAHOT celebrations in 2018 (Luciani 2023: 202). The following year, Laura Luciani explains, the Women's Initiatives Supporting Group chose not to mark IDAHOT, noting that, even if police could be trusted to provide security at the event, doing so would function as a cover for police failure in general to ensure "timely and adequate response to and effective investigation of homo/transphobic hate crime" (202, quoting Women's Initiatives Supporting Group [WISG] 2019). Moreover, issues around police violence in general in Georgia were well-known, with one incident unrelated to LGBT rights having led to weeks of protests in 2019 (10).

Yet the Court's decision reflects ongoing calls by many human rights advocates and institutions for increased training for police, with the hope – in a somewhat circular logic – that over-criminalized communities will gain sufficient trust in the police to report crime. As we saw in Section 2.3 in reference to the policing handbook, police reformists often cite community mistrust as a principal harm of police brutality and other misconduct. A report by ILGA-Europe that the ECtHR quoted in *Identoba* about Georgia's failure to implement its legislation criminalizing homophobic and transphobic hate crimes, for example, specifically noted that the state had not engaged in "training the relevant police officers or [taking] actions to build confidence between law enforcement forces and the LGBT community, in order to allow victims to feel confident enough to report incidents."[106]

The 2022 European Parliament–commissioned report on democratic oversight of policing mentioned in Section 3.1.2 also notes that high-profile police violence cases "can have an adverse effect on public attitudes toward the police" (Guittet et al. 2022: 19, emphasis omitted). Citing a variety of studies across Europe demonstrating that distrust toward police, especially by racial minorities, arises from factors ranging from "poorly handled encounters with the police" to social exclusion and inequality, the report also highlights the impact of negative treatment on the institution of policing itself: "If people feel they are treated fairly and decently, they are more likely to comply with [an] officer's instructions" (20).

Abolitionists faced with the same evidence would take a different tack. They would argue for redistributing resources to address social exclusion and inequality rather than deploying more police and police resources in communities who are already over-criminalized in an effort to make the communities feel as though they are, in the words of the report, "being taken seriously" (Guittet et al. 2022: 20). The report addresses and is sympathetic to the sentiments behind calls to "abolish" and "defund" the police, which it considers after

---

[106] *Identoba* v. *Georgia*, para. 39 (quoting ILGA-Europe 2013: 103).

a section on police brutality. But it arguably undermines these calls by identifying them as merely symptomatic of a loss of confidence in the police and insisting that they can best be responded to through better policing encounters with communities of color (18–21).

Abolitionists have identified this emphasis on training police officers, which is often articulated alongside concerns about lack of trust in the police, as a reformist reform. Indeed, the first question on Mariame Kaba's (2014) "simple guide for evaluating any suggested 'reforms'" of policing in the United States is: "Are the proposed reforms allocating more money to the police? If yes, then you should oppose them." For Critical Resistance (2020a), not only will more training "require more funding and resources going to police to develop and run trainings," but even promoting training "furthers the belief that better training would ensure that we can rely on police for safety, and that instances of police harm and violence occur because of lack of training." In addition, training tends to increase the "tools and tactics available to police as well as their capacity to use them" (Critical Resistance 2020a).

One need not identify as an abolitionist to oppose training as a response to police violence, as the 2022 report by the European Roma Rights Centre (Rorke 2022) demonstrates. The ERRC often intervenes in cases before the ECtHR and was one of the NGOs that argued (successfully) as a third party in *Nachova* that Article 14 imposed a positive obligation on Bulgaria to investigate possible racist motives behind the military police killing of two Roma men. The organization's report importantly dismisses "the standard recourse to racial awareness and diversity training for law enforcement," particularly given that "[i]n the case of police brutality against Roma, the bias at play is very conscious and the prejudice brought to bear is willed and very far from unwitting" (Rorke 2022: 68). Indeed, in its list of recommendations, which it contends comes "as a demand [of European Union member states] that state authorities abide by their declared commitments to the principles of justice and equal protection," the ERRC offers what many abolitionists would consider a non-reformist reform: "Resources dedicated to 'enhancing the training strategies of law enforcement' could be diverted to support Romani communities to advocate for the elimination of racialized policing, to hold the police to account, and to educate and empower members of the community to exercise their rights" (89).

An increasing number of feminists, especially but not only those identifying as abolitionist, now question the dominant response to domestic violence that relies upon increased policing, also calling for funds to be spent elsewhere. Though gaining traction, these insights are not new. As Laureen Snider (2000: 113) argued more than twenty years ago, "policies increasing criminalization virtually guarantee that money will be diverted from feminist shelters, consciousness-raising or empowerment programmes and channelled into criminal justice systems to finance compulsory arrest and/or charge policies."

Many feminists who oppose increased engagement with the police point to the extent to which the very communities who experience over-incarceration are most likely to be subjected to the criminalization of domestic violence. They also commonly note (for example, Goodmark 2021: 10–11; Kaba and Ritchie 2022: 78) that increased police response leads to increased arrests of women, particularly when, as in many parts of the United States, police are required to make an arrest when they have probable cause of domestic violence.

Feminist abolitionists often emphasize that police officers are also perpetrators of domestic violence (as we saw in *A. and B.* v. *Georgia*) and sexual violence. Meiners, nia t. evans, Davis, Dent, and Richie (2022), point out that sexual violence is the second-most reported police misconduct in the United States and that "[p]olice households are more likely to experience domestic violence than the general population." Given that abuse by the police "carries the power and protection of the state," they ask: "Who do you call when the police officer is the rapist? What do you do when calling the cops on your abuser brings violence – not relief – to your door?" These and similar concerns have led a number of feminist abolitionists of color (through INCITE!) to call for anti-police brutality organizers to "be concerned with and invested in developing responses to violence that are not law enforcement based" (INCITE! Women of Color Against Violence 2018: 40).

Feminist opposition to the bill that led to the UK's 2022 Police, Crime, Sentencing and Courts Act, discussed in Section 3.1.1, was partly fueled by public attention to recent police violence against women in the country. This violence included the 2021 rape and murder of Sarah Everard by a Metropolitan police officer in London and extensive use of force by police during a vigil held in her honor. Not only did many feminists (and others) oppose provisions in the act that would make the crackdown on protests easier but they also contended that police violence against women was systemic. In fact, investigations into Everard's murder found that in 2019 and 2020, 160 Metropolitan police officers were accused of sexual misconduct, including sexual assault and sexual harassment (Guittet et al. 2022: 17).

Queer abolitionists similarly oppose attempts to increase police engagement with queer communities, arguing in part that LGBT activists should ally with Black, Indigenous, refugee, and other movements in their work on abolition. Pride parades around the world have become key sites for queer police abolitionists to pursue and demonstrate these alliances. Contestation over the various roles of and responses to police participation in Pride celebrations throughout Europe in 2022 is illustrative.

In Turkey, the police played an active role in enforcing Pride bans across the country, arresting nearly 400 marchers and activists in Istanbul alone (France 24 2022a; Human Rights Watch 2022b). In other countries, police presence was called forth to protect against counter-protesters. For example, in Belgrade, which was host to EuroPride 2022, the Serbian government banned the Pride march planned for September, ostensibly due to far-right nationalist threats. Demonstrators were eventually permitted to march a very short distance (though the government claimed they were simply being escorted to a music event), under heavy police presence. Violent counter-protests ensued, leading to more than five dozen arrests and several police officers being injured (France 24 2022b).

In Tbilisi, Georgia, where LGBT community members had begun in 2019 to organize Pride in lieu of IDAHOT, organizers chose not to march but to hold events in places not open to the public after violent far-right, nationalist protests had led to the canceling of Pride in 2021. That 2022 decision partly reflected a split within the LGBT community related to the question whether to rely on police for protection. As Luciani (2023: 202) explains, this split dates to 2017, with some LGBT advocates believing that their safety was threatened not only by the far-right and the police but by community allies who were "putting more emphasis on individual liberties than on the safety concerns of (more socio-economically vulnerable) queer people." Specifically, these advocates began to refuse pressure to risk their safety and lives through "internationally-sanctioned visibility practices," which they tied to Georgia's attempts to join the EU, and expressed concern that those practices, in addition to being dangerous, might "divert attention from more locally-relevant conversations – for instance, on queer people's socio-economic exclusion" (Luciani 2021).

Even participating in the closed events in Georgia entailed risk. Although the EU encouraged participation, the US Embassy prohibited its employees from participating for security reasons (US Embassy Tbilisi 2022). Eventually, twenty-six counter-protesters were arrested but the events went on, with the United Nations Development Program, the EU delegation to Georgia, and several embassies, including the United States, issuing a joint statement declaring "the successful completion of Pride Week 2022" and expressing "gratitude" to the police for their "successful work in maintaining public order and ensuring safety during the Pride Week events" (Georgia Today 2022, quoting United Nations Development Programme 2022). Giving credit to the very police force that has engaged in brutal violence against LGBT and many other communities in the country for a private event deemed successful because of the arrests of counter-protesters both gives the police undue power and does nothing to shift the underlying threats – either physical or material.

Of course, neither nationalist anti-LGBT sentiments nor the distrust of police by LGBT advocates is limited to Georgia. Also in 2022, Pride organizations in Greece and London called upon police not to march in the parade in uniform. Athens Pride cited ongoing "strained relations" with police following police participation in the killing of a gay activist in 2018 (Neos Kosmos 2022). London Pride claimed that "institutional homophobia is alive and kicking in the Metropolitan police," referencing Scotland Yard's systemic failures in investigating the serial killings of gay men (Batty 2022). Lesbians and Gays Support the Migrants organized a letter giving additional reasons for not allowing uniformed police to march or even to patrol the London march, one of which was "widespread distrust of policing among the LGBTQIA+/Queer community, not just in London but elsewhere," especially by "people of colour and queer migrants" (LGS Migrants 2022).

This letter is in line with (and invokes) approaches elsewhere, such as in Toronto, where the abolitionist No Pride in Policing Coalition (Bain and Kinsman 2022) has argued for moving "beyond limited rights-based politics." Doing so is necessary, it contends, "to adopt an abolitionist politics based on defunding and abolishing policing, carceral and disciplinary institutions right now and on building our own alternatives that create real community safety and address people's social needs" (Bain and Kinsman 2022).

Were human rights advocates and institutions to take seriously the critiques of policing articulated by abolitionists (and others), they would at a minimum stop calling for increased police presence or resources for police as a remedy to human rights violations. As such, they would not promote the harm that increased police presence too often brings, particularly on those groups who are already over-criminalized. They would be forced to find alternative ways of preventing and responding to the harms that the police are supposedly meant to address.

Police abolitionists have detailed myriad possibilities in this regard, some of which – such as decriminalization and transformative justice – overlap with proposals by prison abolitionists. Mariame Kaba and Andrea Ritchie (2022: 177) suggest "removing police from specific tasks, arenas, and spaces" and eliminating "the police units, weaponry, and individual cops who are doing the most harm." The police units they recommend eliminating include "'street crime' units, homeless 'outreach' units, vice squads, [and] anti-protest units" (177). Tom Kemp and Koshka Duff (2020) have provided a number of similar concrete proposals for defunding the police in the United Kingdom, encouraging demands "to disarm police of their guns and tasers, to remove stop and search and strip search powers and to abolish units such as the Territorial Support Group, which exist only to quell social unrest." They cite additional possibilities as well, including the decriminalization of specific acts, the firewalling of public services data from immigration and counter-terrorism enforcement, and ending the UK export of arms.

Kaba and Ritchie (2022: 178) make clear that "the demand to defund the police is the floor, not the ceiling. It is a demand in service of a larger vision, not the totality of the vision." Police abolitionists call for state funds that currently go to policing to be used for social services such as housing and education, as well as for the non-police provision of services such as mental health crisis response that many contend the police are poorly positioned to offer. They also see the importance of non-state responses, with. Kaba and Ritchie pointing to efforts by groups across the United States to "build and strengthen community relationships and infrastructure to create safety without cops at the building, block, neighborhood, and city levels" (242). Thompson (2021: 190) writes of collectives and groups in Germany, one of which she cofounded, who draw "on various methods such as community accountability and transformative justice as politics of care, which challenge all forms of violence." As such, they "demonstrate in important ways that abolition is not just about getting rid of violent institutions or relations, but about building institutions and relations that stand in stark contrast to the politics of violence and death, as they render possible breathing and life" (190).[107]

European human rights advocates could begin to tailor some of these alternatives for the communities with and in which they work, in conversation with those whose lives are most negatively impacted by the police. The ECtHR should encourage directly and indirectly the development and implementation of these alternatives in a variety of ways, as I begin to sketch out in Section 4.

4 Sketching the Contours of an Abolitionist Human Rights Court

As I have referenced along the way, abolitionists have over the past fifty years generated a variety of alternatives to criminal punishment, with the long-term aim of nullifying the need for police and prisons. These alternatives range from the creation of transformative, community-based justice mechanisms to the redistribution of funds away from prisons and policing and toward ensuring broad-based social protections and redressing inequality. Abolitionists have also supported a variety of non-reformist reforms, including the protection of prisoners' rights, while eschewing reforms that extend the state's carceral reach, such as building new prisons.

I believe that many of these alternatives would be useful for the ECtHR to promote in various ways. At the same time, my plea to the Court and those

---

[107] Specifically, Thompson (2021: 190) references the work of Women in Exile, LesMigraS, and the Transformative Justice Kollectiv.

advocates who bring cases before it is relatively modest. I recognize, along with Dorothy Roberts (2019: 91) – who writes in her call for an abolitionist US Supreme Court – that "Court decisions alone will not abolish prisons." They can, however "weaken many of the practices ... that help to reinforce and expand them" (91).

To participate in such weakening, the ECtHR would not need to expand its competencies. Indeed, the Court would need to begin by shrinking some of its capacities, specifically by taking seriously its own oft-repeated claim that it is "not a criminal court" but a human rights court. In multiple instances in which it has held a state accountable for acts for which no one has been held criminally liable, the ECtHR has made clear that its job is not to assess criminal liability "because that responsibility is distinct from international law responsibility under the Convention."[108] This understanding of the Court's role makes good abolitionist sense as it seeks a means of accountability other than criminal law and puts the onus on states to address the harms that give rise to complaints. Yet, the Court belies its claim not to be a criminal court when, as a proxy, it imposes positive obligations on states to police, prosecute, and punish.

The ECtHR is, of course, far from alone among human rights institutions in its turn to criminal law. As the *jus commune* of human rights has developed, the Court has both directly and indirectly borrowed from other institutional bodies that have made the turn. As we have seen in various cases, for instance, the Court has drawn from several UN treaty bodies, particularly the CERD and the CEDAW Committee, in its findings that states have positive obligations to police and punish racialized and gendered violence. (Ironically, perhaps, as Pinto [2023: 116–117] points out, it has chosen not to follow some UN treaty bodies with regard to decriminalization in some areas, including abortion and sex work.)

Yet the ECtHR is in a position to break away from what has become human rights common sense. More than with any other human rights adjudicatory body, judges and other actors engaged with the Court have documented and warned against the Court's deployment of criminal law as a sword. To break away, the ECtHR should harness its own history of wariness of criminal law and even its encouragement of what many consider non-reformist penal reforms. At

---

[108] *Dimitrov and Others* v. *Bulgaria*, App. No. 77938/11 (Eur. Ct. H.R. Jul. 1, 2014), para. 129; *Filipovi* v. *Bulgaria*, App. No. 24867/04 (Eur. Ct. H.R. Apr. 29, 2012), para. 66. For similar assertions by the Court, see *McCann and Others* v. *The United Kingdom*, App. No. 18984/91 (Eur. Ct. H.R. Sep. 27, 1995), para. 173 (Grand Chamber); *Tanlı* v. *Turkey*, App. No. 26129/95 (Eur. Ct. H.R. Apr. 10, 2001), para. 111; *Tekın and Arslan* v. *Belgium*, App. No. 37795/13 (Eur. Ct. H.R. Dec. 5, 2017), para. 81. But see *Giuliani and Gaggio* v. *Italy*, App. No. 23458/02 (Eur. Ct. H.R. Mar. 24, 2011), para. 182 (Grand Chamber) and *Volk* v. *Slovenia*, App. No. 62120/09 (Eur. Ct. H.R. Mar. 13, 2013), para. 106, both finding that the state had not violated the Convention.

the same time, it should affirm its condemnation of gendered and racialized violence and its commitment to holding states accountable for it.

In this section, I outline an abolitionist-oriented pathway for the ECtHR. In doing so, I continue to consider alternatives to policing and prisons – and encourage the Court to do the same – but my main goal is to provide the Court with meaningful alternatives to imposing obligations on states to prosecute, punish, and police as its response to gendered and racialized violence. I will then turn to some broader-based non-reformist penal reforms that the Court could take, which might influence its determination of positive obligations in all cases involving serious human rights violations.

Much of what I propose should be persuasive to (and is even sometimes derived from) those who do not necessarily identify as abolitionist. As we have already seen, many advocates – particularly those working on sexual and gender-based violence and anti-racist, homophobic, and transphobic violence – express concerns about the effects (and effectiveness) of criminalization. Others take a position of penal moderation or minimalism arguing, as Tulkens and Snacken do, that criminal law should be used only as a last resort. Even within these perspectives, we can glean numerous alternatives to the way the Court has been approaching gendered and racialized violence as well as criminalization more generally.

4.1 Holding States Accountable for Gendered and Racialized Violence

Perhaps the most straightforward abolitionist change that the ECtHR could make is to *stop* imposing positive obligations on states to use or ramp up their criminal punishment system to respond to human rights violations. While not requiring criminal punishment would be a necessary first step, it is of course not sufficient. It would fall short of the ECtHR's commitment to preventing and holding states accountable for serious human rights violations, including gendered and racialized violence. The Court should maintain and even reinforce that commitment, but, in Hudson's words (1998: 245), "according to a logic that makes for more effective remedies than either doing nothing (or, at most, very little), or punishing offenders by confining them in settings where their racist and sexist attitudes, and their fantasies of violence and sexuality, will be further fuelled."

The Court should therefore call upon states to use non-penal tools – many already existing – to remedy the structural conditions under which violence occurs as well as to ensure that victims are adequately compensated for their pecuniary and non-pecuniary losses. In terms of structural conditions, the obligations aimed at addressing them are arguably no more onerous on states than are the positive obligations the Court already imposes on states to respond to (and presumably prevent future) serious human rights violations through policing, prosecuting, and punishing. Indeed, at least in the context of gender-based violence, some argue that human rights law already requires positive obligations that extend beyond criminal punishment. Goldscheid and Liebowitz (2015: 305), for example, read the law to require that, in addition to prosecuting and punishing, states have three other "P" obligations that are aimed at addressing structural causes of violence: preventing, protecting against, and providing recourse for acts of violence against women. Though criminal punishment is sometimes justified by these three obligations, states should be required to pursue them through non-punitive means.[109]

Goldscheid and Liebowitz (2015) do not discuss the ECtHR in great detail, but they suggest that it is bound by these "5Ps" and even find them included in a report of the Council of Europe dating back to 2009. And while they do not outright oppose criminalization, they do offer significant critiques of it and express concern that prosecution and punishment too often take the emphasis off, or distort, the other "Ps." As Goldscheid has argued in a solo-authored piece (Goldscheid 2015: 206), even after contending that "explicit criminalization should be a part of states' responses" to marital rape, "laws, policies and programs that advance states' obligations to prevent, protect, and provide redress should be prioritized as well to promote the symbolic and practical interventions needed to support transformational and lasting change." An abolitionist court, of course, could focus explicitly on obligating states to prevent, protect, and provide redress through non-criminal means – without the distraction of obligating states to prosecute and punish or the assumption that prosecution and punishment meets the other obligations.

The ECtHR could impose these obligations in a variety of ways, while also ensuring that states have a fair amount of latitude in their choice of – though not commitment to – non-penal responses. For police violence against racialized and gendered minorities, for example, the Court might impose strict liability on states where there is the requisite proof of the violence. That would hopefully encourage states to take up at least some of the non-reformist reforms that police abolitionists have proposed.

---

[109] Goldscheid and Liebowitz (2015: 316) note with concern that "government's role in prevention programs may have punitive attributes." They provide two examples: First, "'protective' services may be used to remove children from a non-abusive mother for 'witnessing' domestic violence committed by an abuser." Second, "States may cite victim compensation programs that can provide 'redress,' but strict eligibility rules, publicity, and requirements of law enforcement involvement may effectively render redress unavailable."

Were the Court to find that states have violated their obligations to prevent, protect from, or provide redress for gendered or racialized violence – and make it clear that prosecution and punishment cannot be a stand-in for those obligations – litigants and states would necessarily shift their attention to the structural causes of the violence. Particularly by identifying structural causes, the Court would necessarily send a message to the state about how it might prevent liability in the future. The Court could use Article 46, as it sometimes already does to require heightened criminalization in similar cases, to suggest general measures that states should take – including in their allocation of resources – to avoid future liability.

In considering structural causes, the Court should look to areas of law other than criminal law, specifically to the multiple often-backgrounded laws that are implicated in racialized and gendered violence. Mala Htun and Francesca R. Jensenius (2020: 156), for instance, emphasize in the context of violence against women that "[w]omen need a firm structural foundation – resources, land, jobs, social support – to contest, and to exit from, violence and harassment in their daily lives." They then turn to areas of law that should be reformed, such as family, property, and labor law.

Given that so many alternatives proposed to criminalization are community-based, the Court might want to be clear about the limits of what states alone are able to do. Goldscheid and Liebowitz (2015: 344) suggest allowing states to meet their obligations by delegating responses to community-based NGOs. Htun and Jensenius (2020: 156) contend that balanced against aggressive state action (if not necessarily criminalization) in response to violent behavior should be "state restraint to enable the unfolding of social norms that generate legitimate norms and empower women." These NGOs, of course, would need to be committed to non-penal responses, which would be different from the current approaches of the human rights NGOs that regularly appear before the Court in these cases.

The Court should also pay more immediate attention to the victims who come before it, without assuming that criminalization is in fact what they want or need. It could take a page from Mathiesen (2000: 344): "Rather than increasing punishment of the offender with the gravity of the offence, which is basic to the present system, I would propose increased support to the victim with the gravity of the offence. In other words, not a punishment scale for offenders, but a support scale for victims." Mathiesen makes several suggestions for the support of victims who "get nothing out of the present system," which include "[e]conomic compensation (from the state) . . . , shielded places where victims who need protection can get it, support centres for battered women, [and] conflict resolution" (343). Some of these proposals – such as shelters, support centers, and conflict resolution – could be a part of the general measures delineated by the Court under Article 46 or could be implicit in the Court's finding that a state has failed in its obligations to prevent and protect.

The individual measure of economic compensation from the state is a bread-and-butter aspect of the Court's competence, given that ECHR Article 41 provides a mechanism for awarding pecuniary and non-pecuniary damages as a part of just satisfaction.[110] For those amounts to address the needs of the claimants, as well as potentially have a deterrent or even a broader remedial effect, the Court would need to be clear about its rationale for awarding damages, which it has been loath to do.

The Court is often criticized for its lack of transparency about how it determines its award amounts (for example, Fikfak 2020; Ichim 2015; Keller, Heri, and Piskóty 2022). Although the Court is thought to rely generally on detailed tables, rarely tethering damage amounts to what the applicant requests, it has not made those tables public (Fikfak 2020: 349–350). Despite these tables, Keller, Heri, and Piskóty (2022: 5–9) point to routine criticism of the lack of consistency in the grant of awards, including by the Court's own judges.

In addition to being more transparent about how it determines damages, the Court should consider awarding monetary damages that represent the "aggravated" harm that the Court already insists is caused by gendered and racialized violence. In fact, current damage awards indicate that the Court might not see the harms from that violence to be as grave as its jurisprudential reasoning suggests, including in the context of victims it considers vulnerable. Fikfak's study analyzing damage awards under Articles 2, 3, and 5 (Fikfak 2020: 351) demonstrates that, notwithstanding a few cases in which the Court arguably took the victims' vulnerability into account, there was "no significant difference in award between cases in which applicants were qualified as vulnerable and cases in which no vulnerability was reported."

Fikfak (2020: 352) postulates the possibility "that the Court takes the applicant's vulnerability . . . into account only when establishing a violation and that, as a consequence, vulnerable individuals are more likely to have suffered a human rights breach than other individuals." If that were true, however, and the Court were to bring its penal logics to monetary damages, it would seem that judgments that find Article 14 violations, particularly in cases of violence, would result in higher non-pecuniary damages. Significant research would need to be undertaken to determine the extent to which damages in cases of violence involving discriminatory motive differ from those without it, but

---

[110] European Convention on Human Rights Art. 41 reads: "If the Court finds that there has been a violation of the Convention or the Protocols thereto, and if the internal law of the High Contracting Party concerned allows only partial reparation to be made, the Court shall, if necessary, afford just satisfaction to the injured party."

a 2016 study is instructive. That research, aimed at detecting whether there was racism or sexism in the ECtHR's damages awards, found that neither race nor sex seemed determinative of a particular award (Altwicker-Hamori, Altwicker, and Peters 2016: 42).

Although the Court's rules state that it is "inappropriate to accept claims for damages with labels such as 'punitive', 'aggravated' or 'exemplary'" (European Court of Human Rights 2024c: 74), Keller, Heri, and Piskóty (2022: 9) point to arguments, including by judges on the Court, that the Court has in fact awarded punitive damages in a number of cases, even without identifying the awards as such. Fikfak (2018) contends that, regardless of how they are framed, the awards should be higher in general, including for reasons of deterrence. Not only do "the low-level awards ... not take into account the tough route the applicant faces in getting to a violation" but they make states "more willing to risk being taken to the Court, especially when there is a specific social benefit (or utility) to breaching the ECHR" (1109). Further, she suggests that, regardless of the amount of damages it gives and the rubric under which it awards them, the Court should frame the damages as a sanction, based on studies that show that when damage amounts are made public and "interpreted as a 'punishment' or 'sanction,' states are less likely to transgress the rules" (Fikfak 2018: 1106).

Even were the Court to increase damages significantly, in part by channeling its recognition of the aggravated harm of gendered and racialized violence into its determination of just satisfaction, these damages should not lessen attention to the Court's imposition of state obligations aimed at structural changes. As Keller, Heri, and Piskóty (2022) put it in expressing concerns about the monetization or commercialization of human rights, just satisfaction awards should not allow "States to 'buy' their way out of violations" (20).

4.2 Promoting Non-reformist Penal Reforms

As we saw in Section 2.2, the ECtHR has found a number of carceral practices to violate the ECHR. Its decisions in this regard stand in contrast to those of the US Supreme Court, which Roberts (2019: 91) contends largely refrains from finding such violations out of fear that "such a ruling would require 'too much justice'" (quoting *McCleskey* v. *Kemp*, 481 U.S. 279, 339 [1987], Brennan, J., dissenting). The ECtHR should continue and expand some of its work that I have already identified as resonating with abolition. Particularly if it were to cease to impose obligations on states to police, prosecute, and punish, it would be able to bolster the shield function of human rights without the distraction or contradiction of the sword. It could promote or require not only structural and individual remedies for gendered and racialized violence but also non-reformist reforms in those cases challenging carceral practices. Such decisions in this latter group of cases would also function to hone non-reformist reforms that might then be available to states to respond to a wide range of human rights violations.

My proposals here are largely drawn from those resonances described in Section 2, with attention to the critiques or limitations discussed there as dissonances. Beginning with decriminalization, the Court could, as Pinto (2023) argues, be guided by some of the analysis of the 1980 *Report on Decriminalisation*. He proposes that, when "called to consider the compatibility of national criminal law with the Convention," the ECtHR "could engage in more thorough scrutiny of the consequences of criminalisation for effective human rights protection ... [and] regard criminalisation as *prima facie* affecting the enjoyment of human rights" (1130). Although this scrutiny might take the ECtHR out of its comfort zone a bit more than my suggestions in Section 4.1, the Court could approach decriminalization in the way it has treated sodomy laws. Further, Pinto contends that the Court simply needs to be as "proactive as when it is not the lack of penalty but its presence that raises concerns for human rights (1130)." Such scrutiny, of course, would require that individuals or groups bring the claims and that the Court not deploy the margin of appreciation.

The Court, perhaps spurred by advocates, might also mine its history of abolishing the death penalty and irreducible life sentences as a basis for serious consideration of prison and police abolition. Again, Mathiesen (2015: 34–35) considers these earlier abolitionist moments to be "turning points," along with the abolition of slavery, youth prisons, and forced labor. They demonstrate that perceptions and approaches can change; what was once thought of as natural, or commonsensical, might become inconceivable or at least impermissible.

Despite the real concerns about rehabilitation discussed in Section 2.2.3, the Court might use as an abolitionist turning point the commitment it expresses to the possibility of rehabilitation in the irreducible life sentence context. Were it to take seriously both the need for a non-retributive approach to criminal punishment and the failure of states to pursue it, the Court might find itself in alignment with abolition given that, for Eduardo Bautista Duran and Jonathan Simon (2019: 92), rehabilitation and abolition are "competing around the same normative values." Noting that abolitionism emerged at "the height of the rehabilitative penology in both Europe and the U.S.," they contend that once it was shown that, rather than rehabilitating, prisons punished and segregated – neither of which was a common justification being proffered for incarceration – it became possible to argue for complete abolition (92).

At a minimum, this attention to (the lack of) rehabilitation would require the Court to confront its inconsistency in the justifications for punishment it proffers. The reality is that the irreducible life sentence cases are outliers in terms of the Court asserting a rehabilitation rationale. In fact, the Court most often asserts deterrence to justify criminal punishment. The rationale can be found throughout the case law as well as in the arguments of advocates. Yet, some (for example, Lavrysen 2020: 43; Peršak 2020: 154–157) have asserted that, while perhaps an effective rhetorical device, the deterrence claim is more often assumed than demonstrated, even against evidence to the contrary. As Tulkens (2012: 158) put it in justifying the use of criminal law only as a last resort, "the effectiveness, particularly in terms of prevention, attributed to criminal law is a far cry from the reality."

Although the ECtHR often both accepts and promotes a deterrence rationale, it appears to have little appetite to require proof of its efficacy or even engage in discussion about it. Indeed, ECtHR Judge Paul Lemmens has recognized, in response to a call for the Court to require convincing evidence of deterrence (including by Peršak 2020), that assessing "the deterrent effect of a given provision will involve some degree of speculation" (Lemmens and Courtoy 2020: 59). Nevertheless, he and his coauthor insist, the Court "is not in a position to undertake any empirical study in this respect" or "argue on the basis of a given criminology theory" (55). They do not acknowledge that, in fact, the Court already largely depends upon the criminology theory of deterrence.

Lavrysen (2020: 50) notes that the Court also sometimes suggests a retributionist rationale by "considering criminal punishment as the vindication of the victim's value and dignity." Nina Peršak (2020) agrees that retribution might play a greater role in the Court's decision-making process than is normally thought, even when the Court seems to be talking about deterrence. She explains that perhaps the Court's "'effective deterrence' mantra is simply a new phrase, perhaps a more objective and neutral phrase in the lexicon of 'symbolism' or 'expressiveness' of criminal law" (151).

A retribution justification, whether stated or not, would reflect an alignment with the broader carceral turn in human rights law and advocacy. Indeed, some human rights advocates have gained significant traction by arguing that retributive justice is warranted, often invoking victims' desires for that conclusion. Alina Balta (2020) names the Court's positive obligations to prosecute and punish gross human rights violations as "retributive responses," which she supports as restorative measures. She relies largely on statements by victims demanding retribution and on some studies in particular countries that she contends "have repeatedly confirmed that justice for victims [of mass human rights violations] necessarily includes the punishment of perpetrators" (Balta

2020: 76–77). An abolitionist-oriented Court would reject that approach. Even assuming that victims' desires should affect the Court's jurisprudence, other studies have reached different conclusions. As with deterrence, the desires of victims are more often asserted than shown, as Kendall and Nouwen (2014) have demonstrated in relation to the International Criminal Court. And, of course, victims' desires are structured by the possible remedies made available to them. The ECtHR should expand those remedies rather than reproduce the rationale.

One need not be an abolitionist to oppose relying on criminal punishment for its expressive function. Particularly when the expressive justification is used to rebut concerns about criminal law being ineffective, many would oppose it. Peršak quotes Cass Sunstein (1996: 2047), for instance, for the proposition that "good expressivists are also consequentialists" (Peršak 2020: 151). An ECtHR aimed at non-reformist reforms would need to address head-on the consequences of policing and punishment.

To pursue other non-reformist reforms, the Court might follow some of the insights of penal minimalists. For example, Snacken (2022: 44) contends that the ECtHR has already recognized the "inherent humiliation" and "unavoidable level of suffering" caused by incarceration and the "increased evidence of the harms suffered by the families of prisoners."[111] Snacken's strict proportionality test for Article 5 would require states to choose the "lowest degree of humiliation possible," meaning that they would need to "avoid imprisonment whenever possible" (45).

An abolitionist-oriented Court would go further. It would take a closer look at a variety of alternatives to prison sentences that are already in circulation in Europe, some of which, as Renzulli and Snacken indicate (see Section 2.2.4), have resulted from challenges to prison overcrowding. But the Court should consider any alternatives with a critical eye. While some, such as early release or sentence modification, might constitute non-reformist reforms, others are rejected outright by abolitionists as purely reformist in nature. Speaking of electronic monitoring, for instance, Critical Resistance (2021: 454) makes clear that it opposes the expansion of "the imprisonment system into people's homes and into the lives of their loved ones." Snacken (2022: 44–45) recognizes that the community sanctions and fines she supports may "challenge fundamental human rights,"

---

[111] Snacken (2022: 44) cites three cases for the Court's recognition of the "inherent humiliation" and suffering caused by imprisonment: *Costello-Roberts* v. *The United Kingdom*, App. No. 13134/87 (Eur. Ct. H.R. Mar. 25, 1993); *Dougoz* v. *Greece*, App. No. 40907/98 (Eur. Ct. H.R. Mar. 6, 2001); *Tyrer* v. *The United Kingdom*, App. No. 5856/72 (Eur. Ct. H.R. Apr. 25, 1978).

though she is satisfied that they do so less than imprisonment. The Court should not make that compromise.

An abolitionist-oriented ECtHR would also ensure that states seek the participation of those communities most impacted. We have seen that human rights NGOs have played a significant role in a number of cases. ILGA-Europe, for example, appeared as intervenor in several of the hate crimes cases. Its interventions aimed at increased punishment for hate crimes do not reflect the views of queer abolitionists who have long fought against hate crimes legislation. Unlike those abolitionists, ILGA-Europe is a repeat player before the Court and has the resources, including the expertise and clout, to guide the strategy.[112] Given that most abolitionist or other grassroots movements seeking alternatives to penality are not likely to have the time, legal expertise, or money to intervene formally in ECtHR cases, an abolitionist court would need to find other ways to attend to their perspectives, including by encouraging that states work with them as part of their positive obligations.

5 Conclusion

I began this Element by identifying deep, if largely unrecognized, tensions between abolitionist and human rights movements. I conclude with the hope that I have demonstrated the need for those in each movement to better understand those tensions and each other. At the same time, I have aimed to open up new possibilities for strategic alliances between them in pursuit of addressing the structural causes of gendered and racialized violence and promoting non-reformist penal reforms more generally.

I would not have chosen the ECtHR as a site for imagining an abolitionist human rights court were it not for the internal and external critique of the Court's deployment of criminal law as a human rights sword. I have argued, however, that advocates and judges not only need to eliminate the use of the sword; they need to move beyond fortifying the shield by attending to the structural causes of the human rights violations the Court claims that it intends to prevent with criminal law. The abolitionist lens, particularly as applied in the United States with a razor focus on racialized and gendered violence that can never be divorced from the state – including its penal system – offers possibilities for reimagining the approach of the Court. Ironically, perhaps, it provides a basis for encouraging the Court to embrace its status as a human rights, rather than a criminal, court.

---

[112] For a discussion of the role of repeat player NGOs in the ECtHR's case law about violence against women, see Cichowski 2016: 899–900.

Many thoughtful abolitionists before me have outlined alternatives to policing and prisons, which I have sought to give the reader some glimpse of and many sources for throughout this Element. I have primarily set my sights, however, on proposing alternatives to the ECtHR's imposition of positive obligations on states to police, prosecute, and punish. Many of these alternatives should appeal even to those who might not immediately identify as abolitionist but who believe that the Court either has promoted too much penality or has not managed to effect meaningful responses to racialized or gendered violence (or both). I hope to have convinced these groups that the Court should continue to hold states accountable for serious human rights violations by imposing positive obligations (along with meaningful pecuniary and non-pecuniary damages), but that those obligations should not rely on criminal law.

Of course, these same positive obligations might be problematic for those abolitionists who are skeptical of giving the state an outsized role, preferring community-based responses that they believe can best be developed without or beyond the state.[113] Yet, to the extent that, at least in the short term, states allocate resources, the Court has the opportunity to play an important role in ensuring that states distribute them in ways that reflect abolitionist ends.

Abolitionists continually remind us that abolition is a process. As with any institution, the ECtHR will not alone either end gendered and racialized violence or actualize abolition. But, in addition to stopping being an impediment to abolition, it can play a significant role in the facilitation of alternatives to punishment as well as law and policy aimed at structural change. It might even transform human rights law and advocacy in the process.

---

[113] For discussions on the role of the state in abolition, see, for example, Anderson 2021; Gilmore 2022: 224–251; and Maynard 2017.

References

Abdel-Monem, T. (2009). Opuz v. Turkey: Europe's Landmark Judgment on Violence Against Women. *Human Rights Brief*, 17(1), 29–33.

Abolitionist Futures. (2020). Defund the Police: Reformist Reforms vs. Abolitionist Steps for UK Policing. Available from: https://perma.cc/8HJL-ZBNU.

Achiume, T. (2020). Black Lives Matter and the UN Human Rights System: Reflections on the Human Rights Council Urgent Debate. *EJIL:Talk!* (blog of the *European Journal of International Law*), December 15. Available from: https://perma.cc/3HJN-36FG.

Altwicker-Hámori, S., Altwicker, T., and Peters, A. (2016). Measuring Violations of Human Rights: An Empirical Analysis of Awards in Respect of Non-pecuniary Damage under the European Convention on Human Rights. *ZaöRV/HJIL (Zeitschrift für ausländisches öffentliches Recht und Völkerrecht [Journal of Foreign Public Law and International Law]/Heidelberg Journal of International Law)*, 75, 1–51. Available from: https://perma.cc/PS9W-LA3W.

Amnesty International. (1965). *Annual Report, June 1, 1964–May 31, 1965*. Available from: https://perma.cc/BWB8-KZUD.

Amnesty International. (1970). *Annual Report, 1969–1970*. Available from: https://perma.cc/R32Z-FM5J.

Anderson, C. (2003). *Eyes Off the Prize*. Cambridge: Cambridge University Press.

Anderson, W. C. (2021). *The Nation on No Map: Black Anarchism and Abolition*. Chico, CA: AK Press.

Armstrong, S. (2018). Securing Prison Through Human Rights: Unanticipated Implications of Rights-Based Penal Governance. *Howard Journal of Crime and Justice*, 57(3), 401–421.

Aspinwall, C. (2021). Life Without Parole Is Replacing the Death Penalty – But the Legal Defense System Hasn't Kept Up. *Marshall Project*, May 22. Available from: https://perma.cc/PQX9-HZVX.

Bain, B., and Kinsman, G (2022). Context Notes: Abolitionist Pride 2022. *NPPC (No Pride in Policing Coalition)*, July. Available from: https://perma.cc/988L-2ZUE.

Balta, A. (2020). Retribution Through Reparations. In Lavrysen, L., and Mavronicola, N., eds., *Coercive Human Rights: Positive Duties to Mobilise the Criminal Law under the ECHR*. Oxford: Hart, 71–92.

Batty, D. (2022). Uniformed Police Not Welcome at Pride in London, Say Organisers. *Guardian*, June 30. Available from: https://perma.cc/8ZFP-YYH9.

Bautista Duran, E., and Simon, J. (2019). Prison Abolition Discourse: Why It Has Been Missing (And Why It Matters). In Lave, T., and Miller, E., eds., *The Cambridge Handbook of Policing in the United States*. Cambridge: Cambridge University Press, 85–103.

Benenson, P. (1961). The Forgotten Prisoners. Article originally published in *The Observer* and reproduced by Amnesty International's *Speak Free* in 2011. Available from: https://perma.cc/Y2PH-X5TP.

Bernstein, E. (2019). *Brokered Subjects: Sex, Trafficking, and the Politics of Freedom*. Chicago, IL: University of Chicago Press.

Buyse, A. (2009). Landmark Judgment on Domestic Violence. *ECHR Blog*, June 10. Available from: https://perma.cc/8YS3-UEB2.

Cavallaro, J. L., and O'Connell, J. (2020). When Prosecution Is Not Enough: How the International Criminal Court Can Prevent Atrocity and Advance Accountability by Emulating Regional Human Rights Institutions. *Yale Journal of International Law*, 45(1), 1–67.

Celiksoy, E. (2020). "UK Exceptionalism" in the ECtHR's Jurisprudence on Irreducible Life Sentences. *International Journal of Human Rights*, 24(10), 1594–1615.

Charbit, J., and Ricordeau, G. (2021). Prison Abolition Movement in France: Theoretical and Tactical Debates Since the 1970s. In Coyle, M. J., and Scott, D., eds., *The Routledge International Handbook of Penal Abolition*. Abingdon: Routledge, 160–170.

Cichowski, R. (2016). The European Court of Human Rights, Amicus Curiae, and Violence Against Women. *Law & Society Review*, 50(4), 890–919.

Civil Rights Congress (US). (1951). *We Charge Genocide: The Historic Petition to the United Nations for Relief from a Crime of the United States Government Against the Negro People*. Edited W. L. Patterson. New York: Civil Rights Congress. Available from: https://perma.cc/FP2G-F7UF.

Cliquennois, G., Snacken, S., and van Zyl Smit, D. (2021). Can European Human Rights Instruments Limit the Power of the State to Punish? A Tale of Two Europes. *European Journal of Criminology*, 18(1), 11–32.

Council of Europe. (2007). *Factsheet: Death Penalty 2*. Available from: https://perma.cc/4UVJ-W4HN.

Council of Europe. (2022). Opuz v. Turkey 2009: The Landmark Judgment That Inspired Europe to Act on Violence Against Women. Available from: https://perma.cc/7WLB-829X.

Coyle, M. J., and Scott, D., eds. (2021). *The Routledge International Handbook of Penal Abolition*. Abingdon: Routledge.

Crago, A. (2014). "Bitches Killing the Nation": Analyzing the Violent State-Sponsored Repression of Sex Workers in Zambia 2004–2008. *Signs: Journal of Women in Culture and Society*, 39(2), 365–381.

Critical Resistance. (2020a). Reformist Reforms vs. Abolitionist Steps in Policing. *Critical Resistance*, May 14. Available from: https://perma.cc/C2RE-9DEG.

Critical Resistance. (2020b). Reformist Reforms vs. Abolitionist Steps to End Imprisonment. In *Our Communities, Our Solutions: An Organizer's Toolkit for Developing Campaigns to Abolish Policing*, 19. Available from: https://perma.cc/PC7T-KVKZ.

Critical Resistance. (2021). Reformist Reforms vs. Abolitionist Steps in Policing. In Coyle, M. J., and Scott, D., eds., *The Routledge International Handbook of Penal Abolition*. Abingdon: Routledge, 451–455.

Critical Resistance & Incite! ([2001] 2008). Statement on Gender Violence and the Prison Industrial Complex. In CR 10 Publications Collective, ed., *Abolition Now! Ten Years of Strategy and Struggle Against the Prison Industrial Complex*. Oakland, CA: AK Press, 15–29.

Davis, A. Y. (1985). *Violence Against Women and the Ongoing Challenge to Racism*. Latham, NY: Kitchen Table: Women of Color Press.

Davis, A. Y. (2003). *Are Prisons Obsolete?* New York: Seven Stories Press.

Davis, A. Y., Dent, G., Meiners, E. R., and Richie, B. E. (2022). *Abolition. Feminism. Now.* Chicago, IL: Haymarket Books.

Department for the Execution of Judgments of the European Court of Human Rights. (2023). *Life Imprisonment Thematic Factsheet*. Available from: https://perma.cc/HV7F-K8EW.

Deystvie. (2023). Victory for LGBTI+ People in Bulgaria. July 28. Available from: https://perma.cc/Q9HA-YMCK.

Directorate General of Human Rights & Rule of Law, Council of Europe. (2011). *Eradicating Impunity for Serious Human Rights Violations: Guidelines and Reference Texts*. Strasbourg: Council of Europe. Available from: https://perma.cc/CA8A-YQXW.

Dumortier, E., Gutwirth, S., Snacken, S., and De Hert, P. (2011). The Rise of the Penal State: What Can Human Rights Do About It? In Snacken, S., and Dumortier, E., eds. *Resisting Punitiveness in Europe? Welfare, Human Rights and Democracy*. Abingdon: Routledge, 114–124.

Engle, K. (2015). Anti-impunity and the Turn to Criminal Law in Human Rights. *Cornell Law Review*, 100(5), 1069–1128.

Engle, K. (2020). *The Grip of Sexual Violence in Conflict*. Stanford, CA: Stanford University Press.

Engle, K., Miller, Z., and Davis, D. (eds.) (2016). *Anti-impunity and the Human Rights Agenda*. Cambridge: Cambridge University Press.

European Committee on Crime Problems. (1980). *Report on Decriminalisation*. Strasbourg: Council of Europe.

European Court of Human Rights. (2023). *Factsheet – Pilot Judgments*. Available from: https://perma.cc/9WMC-MCQC.

European Court of Human Rights. (2024a). *Guide on Article 46 of the Convention*. Available from: https://perma.cc/ZW7X-M5HX.

European Court of Human Rights. (2024b). *Guide on the Case-Law of the European Convention on Human Rights: Prisoners' Rights*. Available from: https://perma.cc/3Y7H-DVRK.

European Court of Human Rights. (2024c). *Rules of Court*. Available from: https://perma.cc/28FQ-T2PW.

European Union. (2021). *European Union Statement on the Death Penalty at the 1401st Meeting of the Committee of Ministers*. Available from: https://perma.cc/NUC2-QHXQ.

Fair Trials. (2022). *Uncovering Anti-Roma Discrimination in Criminal Justice Systems in Europe*. Available from: https://perma.cc/3HGV-5U9V.

Fassin, D. (2019). The Police Are the Punishment. *Public Culture*, 31(3), 539–561.

Ferrajoli, L. (2000). Sul diritto penale minimo (risposta a Giorgio Marinucci e a Emilio Dolcini). *Il Foro Italiano* 123(4), 125–131.

Fikfak, V. (2018). Changing State Behavior: Damages Before the European Court of Human Rights. *European Journal of International Law*, 29(4), 1091–1125.

Fikfak, V. (2020). Non-pecuniary Damages Before the European Court of Human Rights: Forget the Victim; It's All About the State. *Leiden Journal of International Law*, 33(2), 335–369.

Foucault, M. (2001). Contre les Peines de Substitution. In Foucault, M., *Foucault: Dits et Écrits II, 1976–1988*. Paris: Gallimard, 1024–1026.

Frampton, T. (2022). The Dangerous Few: Taking Seriously Prison Abolition and Its Skeptics. *Harvard Law Review*, 135(8), 2013–2052.

France 24. (2022a). Turkish Police Release All Activists Detained During Istanbul Pride March. *France 24*, June 27. Available from: https://perma.cc/UC4N-77KL.

France 24. (2022b). EuroPride March in Belgrade Marred by Clashes. *France 24*, September 18. Available from: https://perma.cc/MBQ7-LASS.

Francés Lecumberri, P., and Restrepo Rodríguez, D. (2021). Feminist and Other Abolitionist Initiatives in Modern Spain. In Coyle, M. J., and Scott, D., eds.,

The Routledge International Handbook of Penal Abolition. Abingdon: Routledge, 150–159.

Garland, G. (2001). *The Culture of Control*. Chicago, IL: University of Chicago Press.

Georgia Today. (2022). Tbilisi Pride Week 2022 Reviewed. *Georgia Today*, July 7. Available from: https://perma.cc/6S8Z-RAU6.

Gilleri, G. (2023). Sadomasochism in Strasburg: A Pleasurable Danger? *Berkeley Journal of International Law*, 41(1), 39–87.

Gilmore, R. W. (2022). *Abolition Geography: Essays Towards Liberation*. New York: Verso Books.

Gilmore, R. W., and Gilmore, C. (2008). Restating the Obvious, in Indefensible Space: The Architecture of the National Insecurity State. In Sorkin, M., ed., *Indefensible Space: The Architecture of the National Security State*. New York: Routledge, 141–162.

Goldscheid, J. (2015). Considering the Role of the State: Comment on "Criminalizing Sexual Violence Against Women in Intimate Relationships." *American Journal of International Law Unbound*, 109, 202–206.

Goldscheid, J., and Liebowitz, D. (2015). Due Diligence and Gender Violence: Parsing Its Power and Its Perils. *Cornell International Law Journal*, 48(2), 301–345.

Goodmark, L. (2018). *Decriminalizing Domestic Violence: A Balanced Policy Approach to Intimate Partner Violence*. Berkeley: University of California Press.

Goodmark, L. (2021). Gender-Based Violence, Law Reform, and the Criminalization of Survivors of Violence. *International Journal for Crime, Justice and Social Democracy*, 10(4), 13–25.

Gorz, A. (1964). *Stratègie Ouvriére et Nèocapitalisme*. Paris: Editions du Seuil.

Gruber, A. (2020). *The Feminist War on Crime: The Unexpected Role of Women's Liberation in Mass Incarceration*. Berkeley: University of California Press.

Guittet, E., Vavoula, N., Tsoukala, A., and Baylis, M. (2022). *Democratic Oversight of the Police*. Brussels: European Parliament, Policy Department for Citizens' Rights and Constitutional Affairs. Available from: https://perma.cc/A4UD-H8NL.

Gülel, D. (2021). A Critical Assessment of Turkey's Positive Obligations in Combatting Violence Against Women: Looking Behind the Judgments. *Muslim World Journal of Human Rights*, 18(1), 27–53.

Harris, A. (2011). Heteropatriarchy Kills: Challenging Gender Violence in a Prison Nation. *Washington University Journal of Law & Policy*, 37, 13–65.

Heri, C. (2020). Shaping Coercive Obligations Through Vulnerability: The Example of the ECtHR. In Lavrysen, L., and Mavronicola, N., eds., *Coercive Human Rights: Positive Duties to Mobilise the Criminal Law under the ECHR*. Oxford: Hart, 93–116.

Hudson, B. (1998). Restorative Justice: The Challenge of Sexual and Racial Violence. *Journal of Law and Society*, 25(2), 237–256.

Human Rights Watch. (2022a). Turkey Fails to Enforce Court Orders Leaving Women Vulnerable to Abuse. *Human Rights Watch*, June 10. Available from: https://perma.cc/M24Y-JR7H.

Human Rights Watch. (2022b). Turkey: Mass Arrests, Anti-LGBT Violence at Pride. *Human Rights Watch*, June 30. Available from: https://perma.cc/SJK6-X7ZZ.

Huneeus, A. (2013). International Criminal Law by Other Means: The Quasi-criminal Jurisdiction of the Human Rights Courts. *American Journal of International Law*, 107(1), 1–44.

Htun, M., and Jensenius, F. (2020). Fighting Violence Against Women: Laws, Norms, and Challenges Ahead. *Daedalus*, 149(1), 144–159.

Ichim, O. (2015). *Just Satisfaction under the European Convention on Human Rights*. Cambridge: Cambridge University Press.

ILGA-Europe. (2013). Annual Review of the Human Rights Situation of Lesbian, Gay, Bisexual, Trans and Intersex People – 2013: Georgia. *ILGA-Europe*, May. Available from: https://perma.cc/3VVG-SH9G.

ILGA-Europe. (2021). The European Court of Human Rights Finds Croatian Response to Violent Homophobic Attack Fosters Impunity for Hate Crime. *ILGA-Europe*, January 14. Available from: https://perma.cc/KHY9-BJDR.

INCITE! Women of Color Against Violence. (2018). *Law Enforcement Violence Against Women of Color & Trans People of Color: A Critical Intersection of Gender Violence & State Violence*. Redmond, WA: INCITE! Women of Color Against Violence. Available from: https://perma.cc/BS37-R7M6.

Interights. (2022). Opuz v. Turkey. Available from: https://perma.cc/7YF9-JP95.

Jouet, M. (2022). Foucault, Prison, and Human Rights: A Dialectic of Theory and Criminal Justice Reform. *Theoretical Criminology*, 26(2), 202–223.

Kaba, M. (2014). Police "Reforms" You Should Always Oppose. *Truthout*, December 7. Available from: https://perma.cc/AK56-WXTA.

Kaba, M., and Ritchie, A. (2022). *No More Police: A Case for Abolition*. New York: New Press.

Kantack, J. (2019). European Court Slams Russia Over Domestic Violence Case. *Human Rights Watch*, August 22. Available from: https://perma.cc/GET6-ZF43.

Keller, H., Heri, C., and Piskóty, R. (2022). Something Ventured, Nothing Gained? Remedies Before the ECtHR and Their Potential for Climate Change Cases. *Human Rights Law Review*, 22(1), 1–26.

Kemp, T., and Duff, K. (2020). Would "Defund the Police" Work in the UK? *NM (Novara Media)*, June 13. Available from: https://perma.cc/435C-JF3Z.

Kendall, S., and Nouwen, S. (2014). Representational Practices at the International Criminal Court: The Gap between Juridified and Abstract Victimhood. *Law and Contemporary Problems*, 76(3/4), 235–262.

Kilroy, D., and Quixley, S. (2021). A Word Waiting to Happen: Sisters Inside's Abolition Journey. In Coyle, M. J., and Scott, D., eds., *The Routledge International Handbook of Penal Abolition*. Abingdon: Routledge, 21–31.

Kleinstuber, R., Joy, S., and Mansley, E. (2016). Into the Abyss: The Unintended Consequences of Death Penalty Abolition. *University of Pennsylvania Journal of Law and Social Change*, 19(3), 185–206.

Lamble, S. (2011). Transforming Carceral Logics: 10 Reasons to Dismantle the Prison Industrial Complex Using a Queer/Trans Analysis. In Stanley, E. A., and Smith, N., eds., *Captive Genders: Trans Embodiment and the Prison Industrial Complex*. Oakland, CA: AK Press, 235–266.

Lamble, S. (2021). The False Promise of Hate Crime Laws. *Abolitionist Futures*, March 15. Available from: https://perma.cc/BV66-EQ9Q.

Langer, M. (2020). Penal Abolitionism and Criminal Law Minimalism: Here and There, Now and Then. *Harvard Law Review*, 133(9), 42–77.

Lavrysen, L. (2020). Positive Obligations and the Criminal Law: A Bird's-Eye View on the Case Law of the European Court of Human Rights. In Lavrysen, L., and Mavronicola, N., eds., *Coercive Human Rights: Positive Duties to Mobilise the Criminal Law under the ECHR*. Oxford: Hart, 29–54.

Lavrysen, L., and Mavronicola, N. (eds.) (2020). *Coercive Human Rights: Positive Duties to Mobilise the Criminal Law under the ECHR*. Oxford: Hart.

Lazarus, L. (2020). Preventive Obligations, Risk and Coercive Overreach. In Lavrysen, L., and Mavronicola, N., eds., *Coercive Human Rights: Positive Duties to Mobilise the Criminal Law under the ECHR*. Oxford: Hart, 249–266.

Lemmens, P., and Courtoy, M. (2020). Positive Obligations and Coercion: Deterrence as a Key Factor in the European Court of Human Rights' Case Law. In Lavrysen, L., and Mavronicola, N., eds., *Coercive Human Rights: Positive Duties to Mobilise the Criminal Law under the ECHR*. Oxford: Hart, 55–70.

Leskinen, M. (2020). The Istanbul Convention on Sexual Offences: A Duty to Reform the Wording of National Law or the Way We Think? In Niemi, J., Peroni, L., and Stoyanova, V., eds., *International Law and Violence Against*

Women: Europe and the Istanbul Convention. Abingdon: Routledge, 133–156.

Levine, K. (2021). Police Prosecutions and Punitive Instincts. *Washington University Law Review*, 98(4), 997–1057.

LGS Migrants. (2022). No Pride in Cops/No Cops at Pride. June 14. Available from: https://perma.cc/32H8-RX2M.

Librairie des femmes de Milan. (2019). *Ne crois pas avoir de droits: La génération de la liberté féminine à travers les idées et les aventures d'un groupe de femmes*. Bordeaux: Editions la Tempête. Available from: https://editionslatempete.com/produit/ne-crois-pas-avoir-de-droits/.

Lopez, R. (2020). The Law of Gravity. *Columbia Journal of Transnational Law*, 58(3), 565–622.

Luciani, L. (2021). The Perks and Perils of Geopolitical Framings of LGBTQ+ Rights in Georgia. *LSE (London School of Economics and Political Science)*, November 24. Available from: https://perma.cc/Y9U5-DXQM.

Luciani, L. (2023). Where the Personal Is (Geo)Political: Performing Queer Visibility in Georgia in the Context of EU Association. *Problems of Post-Communism*, 70(2), 197–208.

Malby, S. (2019). *Criminal Theory and International Human Rights Law*. Abingdon: Routledge.

Mandela, N. (1995). *Long Walk to Freedom: The Autobiography of Nelson Mandela*. New York: Back Bay Books.

Mathiesen, T. ([1974] 2015). *The Politics of Abolition: Essays in Political Action Theory*. Reprinted in Mathiesen, T., *The Politics of Abolition Revisited*. New York: Routledge, 43–236.

Mathiesen, T. (2000). Towards the 21st Century: Abolition – An Impossible Dream? In West, G., and Morris, R., eds., *The Case for Penal Abolition*. Toronto: Canadian Scholars Press, 333–353.

Mathiesen, T. (2015). *The Politics of Abolition Revisited*. New York: Routledge.

Mavronicola, N. (2014). Inhuman and Degrading Punishment, Dignity, and the Limits of Retribution. *Modern Law Review*, 77(2), 292–307.

Mavronicola, N. (2020). Coercive Overreach, Dilution and Diversion: Potential Dangers of Aligning Human Rights Protection with Criminal Law (Enforcement). In Lavrysen, L., and Mavronicola, N., eds., *Coercive Human Rights: Positive Duties to Mobilise the Criminal Law under the ECHR*. Oxford: Hart, 183–202.

Mavronicola, N., and Lavrysen, L. (2020). Coercive Human Rights: Introducing the Sharp Edge of the European Convention on Human Rights. In Lavrysen, L., and Mavronicola, N., eds., *Coercive Human Rights: Positive Duties to Mobilise the Criminal Law under the ECHR*. Oxford: Hart, 1–28.

Maynard, R. (2017). *Policing Black Lives: State Violence in Canada from Slavery to the Present*. Halifax, NS: Fernwood.

McLeod, A. (2019). Envisioning Abolition Democracy. *Harvard Law Review*, 132(6), 1613–1649.

McQuigg, R. (2021a). Domestic Abuse as Torture? Recent Jurisprudence of the European Court of Human Rights. *QPOL (Queen's Policy Engagement)*, December 21. Available from: https://perma.cc/6V5N-J9VL.

McQuigg, R. (2021b). The European Court of Human Rights and Domestic Violence: Volodina v. Russia. *International Human Rights Law Review*, 10(1), 155–167.

Mégret, F., and Calderón, J. S. (2015). The Move towards a Victim-Centred Concept of the Criminal Law and the "Criminalization" of Inter-American Human Rights Law: A Case of Human Rights Law Devouring Itself? In Haeck, Y., Ruiz-Chiriboga, O., and Burbano-Herrera, C., eds., *The Inter-American Court of Human Rights: Theory and Practice, Present and Future*. Cambridge: Intersentia, 419–442.

Meijer, S. (2017). Rehabilitation as a Positive Obligation. *European Journal of Crime, Criminal Law and Criminal Justice*, 25, 145–162.

Meiners, E. R., evans, n. t., Davis, A. Y., Dent, G., and Richie, B. E. (2022). Why Policing and Prisons Can't End Gender Violence. *Boston Review*, January 24. Available from: https://perma.cc/MH9B-HAWC.

Mogul, J. (2015). Lawyer for Chicago Torture Victims: A Model for Responding to Police Brutality. *Time*, May 12. Available from: https://perma.cc/7VKW-DC7G.

Murdoch, J., and Roche, R. (2013). *The European Convention on Human Rights and Policing: A Handbook for Police Officers and Other Law Enforcement Officials*. Strasbourg: Council of Europe. Available from: https://perma.cc/MQF2-CW7H.

Neos Kosmos. (2022). *Greek Politicians Present at Athens Pride, LGBT Police Told to Participate Without Uniform*. Neos Kosmos, June 19. Available from: https://perma.cc/LF8E-A4QZ.

Niemi, J., and Sanmartin, A. (2020). The Concepts of Gender and Violence in the Istanbul Convention. In Niemi, J., Peroni, L., and Stoyanova, V., eds., *International Law and Violence Against Women: Europe and the Istanbul Convention*. Abingdon: Routledge, 77–94.

Office of the High Commissioner for Human Rights (OHCHR). (2022). Experts of the Committee on the Elimination of Racial Discrimination Commend the United States of America on the COVID-19 Hate Crimes Act, Ask About Absence of a National Human Rights Institute and Measures to Address Gun

Violence. *United Nations OHCHR*, August 12. Available from: https://perma.cc/F9NY-6KF4.

O'Loughlin, A. (2021). Risk Reduction and Redemption: An Interpretive Account of the Right to Rehabilitation in the Jurisprudence of the European Court of Human Rights. *Oxford Journal of Legal Studies*, 41(2), 510–538.

Olufemi, L. (2021). *Feminism Interrupted: Disrupting Power*. London: Pluto Press.

Parla, A. (2019). *Precarious Hope: Migration and the Limits of Belonging in Turkey*. Stanford, CA: Stanford University Press.

Peroni, L., and Timmer, A. (2013). Vulnerable Groups: The Promise of an Emerging Concept in European Human Rights Convention Law. *International Journal of Constitutional Law*, 11(4), 1056–1085.

Peršak, N. (2020). Positive Obligations in View of the Principle of Criminal Law as a Last Resort. In Lavrysen, L., and Mavronicola, N., eds., *Coercive Human Rights: Positive Duties to Mobilise the Criminal Law under the ECHR*. Oxford: Hart, 141–160.

Petrova, D. (2013). Evolving Strasbourg Jurisprudence on Domestic Violence: Recognising Institutional Sexism. *Oxford Human Rights Hub*, June 20. Available from: https://perma.cc/85JH-SNHP.

Pinto, M. (2018). Awakening the Leviathan Through Human Rights Law – How Human Rights Bodies Trigger the Application of Criminal Law. *Utrecht Journal of International and European Law*, 34(2), 161–184.

Pinto, M. (2020). Sowing a "Culture of Conviction": What Shall Domestic Criminal Justice Systems Reap from Coercive Human Rights? In Lavrysen, L., and Mavronicola, N., eds., *Coercive Human Rights: Positive Duties to Mobilise the Criminal Law under the ECHR*. Oxford: Hart Publishing, 161–182.

Pinto, M. (2023). Coercive Human Rights and the Forgotten History of the Council of Europe's Report on Decriminalisation. *Modern Law Review*, 86(5), 1108–1133.

Reappropriate. (2021). 100+ Asian and LGBTQ Organizations' Statement in Opposition to Law-Enforcement-Based Hate Crime Legislation. *Reappropriate*, May 12. Available from: https://perma.cc/K5UC-RMAZ.

Renzulli, I. (2022). Prison Abolition: International Human Rights Law Perspectives. *International Journal of Human Rights*, 26(1), 100–121.

Richie, B. (2012). *Arrested Justice: Black Women, Violence, and America's Prison Nation*. New York: New York University Press.

Ritchie, A., Smith, D., Johnson, J., Ifetayo, J., Stahly-Butts, M., Kaba, M., Simmons, M., Taifa, N., Herzing, R., Wallace, R., and Obuya, T. (2022).

Reparations Now Toolkit. Edited A. Ritchie and M. Stahly-Butts. M4BL (Movement for Black Lives). Available from: https://perma.cc/F597-7S7A.

Roberts, D. (2019). The Supreme Court 2018 Term: Foreword: Abolition Constitutionalism. *Harvard Law Review*, 133(1), 1–122.

Rodriguez, S. M. (2021). Queer Abolitionist Alternatives to Criminalising Hate Violence. In Coyle, M. J., and Scott, D., eds., *The Routledge International Handbook of Penal Abolition*. Abingdon: Routledge, 190–200.

Rorke, B. (2022). *Brutal and Bigoted: Policing Roma in the EU*. Brussels: European Roma Rights Centre.

Ryan, M. (1978). *The Acceptable Pressure Group – Inequality in the Penal Lobby: A Case Study of the Howard League and RAP*. Farnborough: Saxon House.

Ryan, N., and Ward, T. (2014). Prison Abolition in the UK: They Dare Not Speak Its Name? *Social Justice*, 41(3), 107–119.

Scott, D. (2016). Regarding Rights for the Other: Abolitionism and Human Rights from Below. In Weber, L., Fishwick, E., and Marmo, M., eds., *The Routledge International Handbook of Criminology and Human Rights*. Abingdon: Routledge, 50–60.

Seibert-Fohr, A. (2009). *Prosecuting Human Rights Violations*. Oxford: Oxford University Press.

Simon, J. (2019). For a Human Rights Approach to Reforming the American Penal State. *Journal of Human Rights Practice*, 11(2), 346–356.

Sinnar, S. (2022). Hate Crimes, Terrorism, and the Framing of White Supremacist Violence. *California Law Review*, 110, 489–565.

Sinnar, S., and Colgan, B. (2020). Revisiting Hate Crimes Enhancements in the Shadow of Mass Incarceration. *New York University Law Review Online*, 95, 149–170.

Snacken, S. (2022). The European Court of Human Rights and National Policies: Fostering Quantitative and Qualitative Penal Moderation Through Articles 3 and 5 ECHR. In Cliquennois, G., ed., *The Evolving Protection of Prisoners' Rights in Europe*. Abingdon: Routledge, 37–50.

Snider, L. (2000). Towards Safer Societies: Punishment, Masculinities and Violence Against Women. In Morris, R., and West, W., eds., *The Case for Penal Abolition*. Toronto: Canadian Scholars Press, 111–163.

Stanley, E., Spade, D., and Queer (In)Justice. (2012). Queering Prison Abolition, Now? *American Quarterly*, 64(1), 115–127.

Stavros, S. (2020). Criminal Law Responses to Hate Speech: Towards a Systematic Approach in Strasbourg. In Lavrysen, L., and Mavronicola, N., eds., *Coercive Human Rights: Positive Duties to Mobilise the Criminal Law under the ECHR*. Oxford: Hart, 117–140.

Sunstein, C. (1996). On the Expressive Function of Law. *University of Pennsylvania Law Review*, 144, 2021–2053.

Szydło, M. (2012). Vinter v. United Kingdom. *American Journal of International Law*, 106(3), 624–630.

Tapia Tapia, S. (2024). An Anticolonial, Abolitionist, and Feminist Lens to Interrogate Human Rights Penality. In Weber, L., and Marmo, M., eds., *A Research Agenda for a Human Rights Centred Criminology*. Cham: Palgrave Macmillan, 97–110.

Thibaud, P. (1979). Toujours les prisons. *Esprit*, 11, 3–9.

Thompson, V. (2021). Beyond Policing: For a Politics of Breathing. In Duff, K., ed., *Abolishing the Police*. London: Dog Section Press, 179–191.

Thornberry, P. (2016). *The International Convention on the Elimination of All Forms of Racial Discrimination: A Commentary*. Oxford: Oxford University Press.

Trotter, S. (2022). Hope's Relations: A Theory of the "Right to Hope" in European Human Rights Law. *Human Rights Law Review*, 22(2), 1–21.

Tulkens, F. (2011). The Paradoxical Relationship between Criminal Law and Human Rights. *Journal of International Criminal Justice*, 9(3), 577–595.

Tulkens, F. (2012). Human Rights as the Good and the Bad Conscience of Criminal Law. In Snacken, S., and Durmotier, E., eds., *Resisting Punitiveness in Europe? Welfare, Human Rights and Democracy*. Abingdon: Routledge, 156–175.

Tulkens, F. (2020). Foreword. In Lavrysen, L., and Mavronicola, N., eds., *Coercive Human Rights: Positive Duties to Mobilise the Criminal Law under the ECHR*. Oxford: Hart, v–x.

United Nations Committee on the Elimination of Racial Discrimination (CERD). (2022). CERD/C/USA/CO/10–12: Concluding Observations on the Combined Tenth to Twelfth Reports of the United States of America. *United Nations OHCHR*, September 21. Available from: https://perma.cc/GG7N-BTVK.

United Nations Development Programme (UNDP). (2022). Pride Week 2022: A Potential Stepping-Stone for Enhancing LGBTQI+ Rights Protection in Georgia. *UNDP*, July 6. Available from: https://perma.cc/E7UL-5Q9P.

US Embassy Tbilisi. (2022). Security Alert: U.S. Embassy Tbilisi, Georgia. *US Embassy in Georgia*, June 28. Available from: https://perma.cc/QZG5-WSRC.

van Zyl Smit, D., and Appleton, C. (2019). *Life Imprisonment: A Global Human Rights Analysis*. Cambridge, MA: Harvard University Press.

Vergès, F. (2022). *A Feminist Theory of Violence: A Decolonial Perspective*. Translated M. Thackway. London: Pluto Press.

Wallace, A. (2020). The European Court of Human Rights: A Tool for Improving Human Rights. *Lancet Public Health*, 5(2), 78–79.

Walters, M., and Tumath, J. (2014). Gender "Hostility," Rape, and the Hate Crime Paradigm. *Modern Law Review*, 77(4), 563–596.

Weber, B. (2021). Anticarceral Internationalism: Rethinking Human Rights Through the Imprisoned Black Radical Tradition. *Journal of African American History*, 106(4), 706–735.

Wild, B. (2016). ECtHR Cases with Criminal Law Implications. *New Journal of European Criminal Law*, 7(3), 370–380.

Women's Initiatives Supporting Group (WISG). (2019). WISG's Statement for May 17. Available from: https://perma.cc/6HSE-T6Z2.

Wong, W. H. (2012). *Internal Affairs: How the Structure of NGOs Transforms Human Rights*. Ithaca, NY: Cornell University Press.

Working Chance. (2021). Joint Statement: The Police, Crime, Sentencing and Courts Bill Will Have Harmful Long-Term Consequences for Women. *Working Chance blog, policy briefing*, July 5. Available from: https://perma.cc/3U3R-9BX4.

X, M. (1965). The Ballot or the Bullet, April 3rd, 1964, Cleveland. In Breitman, G., ed., *Malcolm X Speaks: Selected Speeches and Statements*. New York: Grove Press, 23–44.

Zimmerman, N. (2015). Legislating for the Vulnerable? Special Duties under the European Convention of Human Rights. *Swiss Review of International and European Law*, 25, 539–562.

Zurn, P., and Dilts, A. (2016). *Active Intolerance: Michel Foucault, the Prisons Information Group, and the Future of Abolition*. New York: Palgrave Macmillan.

Acknowledgments

For their generous feedback on various drafts of this Element, I am grateful to Arnulf Becker Lorca, Cooper Christiancy, Richard Clements, Laurel Fletcher, Vanja Hamzić, Fleur Johns, Nadia Lambek, Natasa Mavronicola, Zinaida Miller, Val Moghadam, Sarah Nouwen, Mattia Pinto, and students and colleagues in sessions at Harvard Law School, Northeastern University School of Law, SOAS School of Law, Tulane University Law School, UC Berkeley School of Law, University of Birmingham Law School, and UNSW Sydney Faculty of Law and Justice. Many thanks to Neville Hoad, my co-director of the Rapoport Center for Human Rights and Justice at the University of Texas, for co-organizing with me the Center's 2019 conference on "Prison Abolition, Human Rights, and Penal Reform." Many of the ideas in the book were sparked by conversations with him, Aziza Ahmed, Ruth Wilson Gilmore, Sarah Lamble, Frédéric Mégret, Zinaida Miller, Vasuki Nesiah, and other participants at the event. I am also enormously grateful to Maria Ximena Davila for her outstanding research assistance and dialogue with me about the project over the past three years. In addition, I appreciate the research assistance of Angelina Bishman, Liz Castillo, and Ian K. Miller.

Cambridge Elements

International Law and Society

Richard Clements
Tilburg University

Richard Clements is an Assistant Professor of International Law at Tilburg Law School in the Netherlands. His research primarily concerns the interconnections between international legal thought, managerial ideas and practices, and the changing styles of international legal expertise.

Luis Eslava
La Trobe University

Luis Eslava is a Professor of International Law at La Trobe University, Australia. Luis' interdisciplinary research straddles the fields of international law, international legal history and theory, and international development, with a particular focus on the global legal and economic order and its relation to precarity and violence in the Global South.

Markus Gunneflo
Lund University

Markus Gunneflo is an Associate Professor of Public International Law at Lund University, Sweden. Markus researches the theory and history of international law, focusing on inequalities—especially in a North-South dimension—in the context of use of force, international humanitarian law, human rights, development, migration, the law of outer space, and more.

Nadia Lambek
Western University

Nadia Lambek is an Assistant Professor at Western University Faculty of Law in Canada. Her research explores international law's constitutive role in shaping the "rural" and global food systems, social movement engagement with and resistance to international law-making, the mobilization of international legal expertise, and the law of work.

About the Series

Cambridge Elements in International Law and Society offers a platform for cutting-edge interdisciplinary explorations of international law related to social, economic, political, technological, cultural, biological, biophysical and environmental developments across the planet. Operating at the intersection of international legal scholarship and socio-legal studies, this series explores a wide range of topics and deploys different methodological perspectives to the past, present and future of international law. It also offers complex and nuanced approaches to the concepts of law and society in a global context, drawing on theoretically informed and empirically grounded research. Individual volumes provide direct, rapid interventions to emerging debates in international law and society or engage with international law's connection to activism, practice or teaching and the changing styles, arguments and narratives that power the world's legal regimes. They may also offer a masterclass in a specific approach or method.

Cambridge Elements

International Law and Society

Elements in the Series

Toward an Abolitionist Human Rights Court: Rethinking Responses to Gendered and Racialized Violence
Karen Engle

A full series listing is available at: www.cambridge.org/EILS

For EU product safety concerns, contact us at Calle de José Abascal, 56–1°, 28003 Madrid, Spain or eugpsr@cambridge.org.

www.ingramcontent.com/pod-product-compliance
Lightning Source LLC
LaVergne TN
LVHW022040260326
834688LV00061B/1662